THIS IS OUR CONSTITUTION

This Is Our Constitution

DISCOVER AMERICA WITH A GOLD STAR FATHER

KHIZR KHAN

WITH ANNE QUIRK

ALFRED A. KNOPF　　NEW YORK

THIS IS A BORZOI BOOK PUBLISHED BY ALFRED A. KNOPF

Text copyright © 2017 by Khizr Khan
Jacket art copyright © 2017 by R. Kikuo Johnson

Visit us on the Web! rhcbooks.com

Educators and librarians, for a variety of teaching tools, visit us at
RHTeachersLibrarians.com

Library of Congress Cataloging-in-Publication Data is available upon request.
ISBN 978-1-5247-7091-4 (trade) — ISBN 978-1-5247-7092-1 (lib. bdg.) —
ISBN 978-1-5247-7093-8 (ebook)

The text of this book is set in 11.6-point Garth Graphic Pro.

Printed in the United States of America
October 2017
10 9 8 7 6 5 4 3 2 1

First Edition

* * *

I dedicate this book to all our nation's
middle school students and their teachers—
and especially to our friends in Mr. Merrick's civics
class at the Peabody School in Charlottesville.
Your curiosity about our founding documents
inspired us to write it. You are our heroes.

CONTENTS

The Blessings of Liberty 1

CHAPTER 1 Why We Need a Constitution. 9

CHAPTER 2 Writing the Constitution. 37

CHAPTER 3 Understanding the Constitution. . . . 65

CHAPTER 4 Perfecting the Constitution. 123

CHAPTER 5 The Declaration of Independence
and the Constitution of the United States. 155

Standing with the Constitution 201

More Landmark Supreme Court Cases 206

Acknowledgments 211

Picture Credits and Notes 213

Index 215

THE BLESSINGS OF LIBERTY

Our nation has always looked toward the future. History matters, of course, but the founding documents of the United States are more than history lessons. They point the way forward to a more free, more peaceful, and more just nation. They challenge each generation to build a better United States.

It's all there at the beginning of the Constitution, the Preamble. The framers of the Constitution thought hard about every word, and they could see far down the road, too. When they sought to "secure the Blessings of Liberty to ourselves and our Posterity," they were talking about you. *You* are the posterity for whom they gathered in Philadelphia. *You* are the future they envisioned.

I know the Constitution will endure because I've seen the dignity and the decency of the American people. My wife and I were privileged to raise three fine boys in this great nation.

If you've always lived in a country that is ruled by laws, and not by dictators, it's hard to imagine living without justice, without even any hope for justice. If you've always had freedom of speech—the right to speak your mind and openly share your opinions—you probably can't imagine what it's like to know that one wrong word could send you to prison for the rest of your life.

I know these fears because I lived with them. I treasure my American citizenship now, but I didn't grow up with it. I was born in Pakistan in 1950. Located in South Asia, between India and Afghanistan, Pakistan was a newly independent country back then, recently separated from England after nearly two hundred years of British rule. Like many newly liberated nations, Pakistan lacked sound government and sound public services and suffered from public corruption. No one trusted the police. The justice system protected the rich (who bribed their way through it) and terrorized the poor. Journalists went to jail for criticizing the military dictators. You could be arrested for attending a protest rally. You could disappear. You could be killed.

My wife, Ghazala Khan, and I came to America because we wanted to live in freedom. We wanted our children to grow up with the blessings of liberty. And they did.

Of course, our boys groaned every time we made yet another visit to yet another monument in Washington, D.C., and rolled their eyes when their mother and I sang the praises of the Bill of Rights at the dinner table—"Enough already, Baba! You've said the same thing thirty times!" But they were paying attention. Our faith in America took root in a new generation.

Humayun Khan, our middle son, studied at the University of Virginia, which was founded by Thomas Jefferson. There, he volunteered for the Army Reserve Officers' Training Corps (ROTC) because he had a deep desire to serve his country. He believed, as he wrote in a college essay, that sacrifice and vigilance were crucial to liberty and democracy. After graduating in 2000, he joined the army, with plans to eventually attend law school and become a military lawyer. One day in 2004, while serving in Iraq, he ordered his fellow soldiers to hit the ground when he walked toward a speeding taxi armed with bombs. He was killed. His fellow soldiers survived. At the age of twenty-seven, he sacrificed his own life to save the lives of others.

Like so many other brave Americans who have died in service to the United States, our son was a hero. We are moved and humbled by his commitment to our nation. We know how much he loved this country.

The spirit of our democracy, the values to which our son dedicated his life, can be seen in the founding documents of the United States, especially the Declaration of Independence and the Constitution. They express the moral principles that to this day guide our legal and political systems. They are idealistic, and they are also practical. Our founders knew that a house can't be built on sand, and that a country can't thrive without a sound government.

But it's also true that our government can't function as intended without informed citizens, especially informed *young* citizens. The Constitution needs each and every one of us to stand with it. Our future depends on *you*—on your commitment to justice and your dedication to liberty.

The Constitution of the United States has endured for more than 225 years—a remarkable achievement.

While many other countries have wholly altered their governments or entirely rewritten their constitutions during times of social or political unrest, our Constitution is resilient and flexible enough to ride out periods of change and to expand our commitment to justice and equal protection.

In 2016, a wave of hate speech directed against my religion, Islam, broke across the country, and certain politicians encouraged ugly prejudices. Many, including some of the children in my neighborhood, began to fear for their safety and the safety of their friends. They had heard reports that Muslim families wouldn't be allowed into the United States anymore. They feared that Muslim families would be sent away from America. Parents brought these children to talk to me because I am a lawyer, a person of faith, and a man who is known to carry a copy of the Constitution in his pocket. I tried to assuage their fears by telling the children about the justice and strength of our founding documents.

Then one day, much to our surprise, my wife and I were invited to make a speech about our son Captain Khan at the Democratic National Convention, the gathering at which the Democratic Party chooses its candidates for president and vice president. It would be a public speech at a televised gathering, and we have always been private people. We knew we would be thrust into the limelight, and we were not sure we were ready for it. We asked for time to decide, and we thought and thought at our home in Charlottesville, Virginia, unsure about what to do. Then I went to check the mail. A note in a child's handwriting was in our mailbox. It said:

"We love Maria. She is our friend. Don't let them throw her out of this country."

We made our decision then and there. We wanted to speak out, as patriotic American Muslims, for all of the freedoms that are enshrined in our Constitution. We wanted to remind our fellow citizens, and the friends of Maria, that we all have rights and we are all equally protected under the law.

Our lives took a sharp turn after our appearance at the Democratic National Convention. Reporters knocked on our door, television producers called, letters arrived from all over the country—and the world. We were asked to speak at conferences and join in debates. The attention can be uncomfortable, but we are honored to stand with everyone who cherishes our fundamental rights as American citizens.

Every day I'm inspired by all the young Americans who call out injustice, insist upon equal rights, push back against bullies, stay informed about public issues, and perform countless acts of kindness and courage. This is patriotism.

It's not always easy, but our responsibility is clear. What I come back to—what I have always come back to—is the short but powerful document that embodies ideals of human dignity and provides a road map for governing our nation. The Constitution is America's beating heart. The Constitution is *yours*. *You* bring it to life. *You* defend it. Without your involvement, it's just words on parchment.

You are my heroes: you are the custodians of the Constitution, and of our country's values and future. It is my privilege to put this book into your blessed hands. It is my fervent hope that its message of freedom, liberty, and fairness will stay with you for the rest of your life and that you will share it with generations to come.

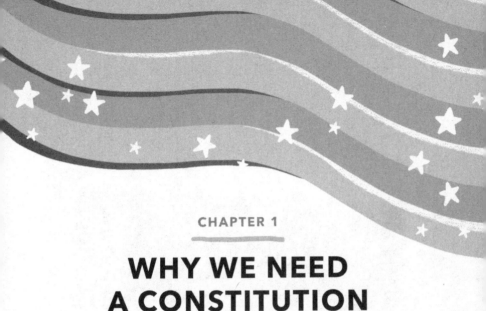

CHAPTER 1

WHY WE NEED A CONSTITUTION

Thomas Jefferson and I were born two hundred years and half a world apart, but we're neighbors now. All that separates his home from ours is a few miles, just a short drive along Route 20 in Virginia, also known as the Constitution Route.

Monticello, the elegant estate that Jefferson designed and called home for more than fifty years, sits on top of Carter Mountain in Charlottesville. Our house, much smaller and far less famous, sits at the foot of Carter Mountain. We are privileged to live so close to greatness, but it's fitting that Jefferson had the better view.

He was a farsighted man, like all our Founding Fathers, and when he looked out on America, he saw its goodness and promise. He devoted his life to creating a nation that respected dignity and rewarded hard work.

Thomas Jefferson's estate, just up the hill from my home in Charlottesville, Virginia.

One of Jefferson's greatest legacies is the Declaration of Independence, which announced, in 1776, that America was no longer a colony of England but a fully free and independent country.

"We hold these truths to be self-evident," the young lawyer wrote, "that all men are created equal, that they are endowed by their Creator with certain unalienable

Rights, that among these are Life, Liberty and the pursuit of Happiness."

Read that sentence out loud. It's a revolutionary statement: both a proclamation of faith in human equality and a firm rebuke of tyranny. It says that people can make decisions about their own lives—no one else has the right to do that for them.

This vision of equality has been hard to realize. Our Founding Fathers made mistakes, some of them appalling. Today, it's possible—and important—to look back and see the many wrong turns in our nation's history, but the ideals set forth in the Declaration of Independence will always be the core values of the United States.

A major part of what became America had been under English rule for 150 years when it declared its independence in 1776. It had been forced to obey a king who had never set foot on American soil and to pay taxes to a government that ignored its needs. This was unjust, insisted Jefferson and his colleagues at the Continental Congress in Philadelphia. It was time for Americans to govern themselves. It was time for America to be free.

"The history of the present King of Great Britain," the Declaration noted, "is a history of repeated injuries and usurpations, all having in direct object the establishment of an absolute Tyranny over these States."

Jefferson's words set a hook in my heart when I first read them as a law student in Pakistan. Just like the United States, Pakistan had been a colony of England, and the people of Pakistan also had a long list of grievances against their British rulers. Although King George III, the king whom Jefferson described as a tyrant, had been dead for over 125 years, the damage done by the governments of his successors could still be felt in Pakistan.

But I was also aware of the damage that Pakistan was doing to itself. Unlike America, Pakistan was not a democratic country. Military dictators had forced their will on the people. Ordinary citizens had no power, no voice in their government.

How had America become a democratic nation that was governed by the rule of law, through free and fair elections, and not a military dictatorship? And how had it preserved, and even strengthened, its founding principles?

The signers of the Declaration of Independence vowed to stand together in 1776. They agreed to "pledge to each other our Lives, our Fortunes and our sacred Honor." But the men who made those promises were long gone by the time I first encountered their words. How had their values been passed down from one generation to the next— and the next and the next, for centuries?

> What a blessing to live in a country governed by the rule of law. Sometimes it takes someone born without such a legacy to humbly remind us how precious it is.

The answer, I realized, was the United States Constitution.

The Constitution is where the promises of the Declaration of Independence are transformed into the legal principles of a representative democracy. It's where Jefferson's complaints against an overreaching and out-of-touch monarch are answered by the creation of a government with clear responsibilities and firm limits. It's where a nation that is ruled by laws, not by commands, finds its structure.

THE STRUCTURE OF THE UNITED STATES GOVERNMENT

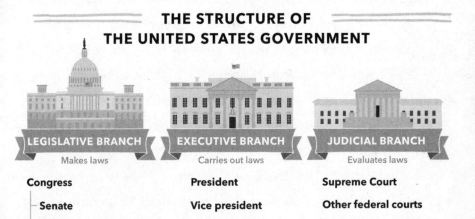

LEGISLATIVE BRANCH	EXECUTIVE BRANCH	JUDICIAL BRANCH
Makes laws	Carries out laws	Evaluates laws
Congress	**President**	**Supreme Court**
Senate	**Vice president**	**Other federal courts**
House of Representatives	**Cabinet**	

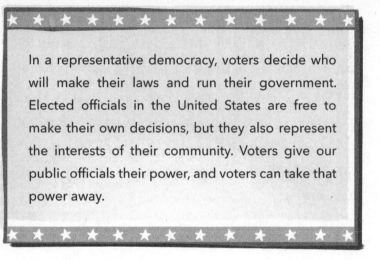

In a representative democracy, voters decide who will make their laws and run their government. Elected officials in the United States are free to make their own decisions, but they also represent the interests of their community. Voters give our public officials their power, and voters can take that power away.

Our Constitution has never been perfect, nor has our nation. As you'll read in the next chapter, shameful compromises were made when the Constitution was being drafted in 1787. Enslaved Americans were denied basic human dignities; they were dehumanized and treated not as people but as property. But the framers were wise enough to give future generations the power to amend the document—to right old wrongs and find new ways to honor our highest ideals. The Constitution is where Jefferson's assertion that "all men are created equal" begins its slow journey from poetry into practice.

Every word in the Constitution is important, and this book will be looking at all of them. It will go back in time to 1787, when the original document was written. It will explore the meaning of the Constitution, article by article, section by section. It will discuss the ways the Constitution has been interpreted—and reinterpreted, and even changed—over the years. It will encourage you to see your role in preserving our Constitution for the future. And it will show you how our nation's founding documents aren't just a blueprint for government—they are the moral basis for the nation. They provide guidance on how we should conduct ourselves as members of a community: a family, a school, a town, all together as a nation.

Perhaps most important, this book includes the full text of both the Declaration of Independence and the Constitution.

I want to turn now to my two favorite sections of the Constitution: the First Amendment and the Fourteenth Amendment. "Amendment" is a legal-sounding word with a very simple meaning. It means "a change." Our Constitution was designed to accommodate change over time, to adapt to new challenges and circumstances. Article V of the Constitution, which was written in 1787, is very clear: new sections could be added.

These additions—these amendments—were intended to be part of the Constitution, and are just as important as every other part of it.

My own copy of the Constitution came with me to the Democratic National Convention in Philadelphia in 2016. I wound up taking it out of my pocket during our speech, though I hadn't originally planned on it. Then I realized that I had to: our Constitution was the real message that night. Today, that copy of the Constitution has a permanent home in the collection of the Virginia Historical Society.

The First Amendment was added in 1791, along with nine other amendments; together, they are commonly called the Bill of Rights. (In future chapters, we'll go more deeply into the Bill of Rights and its crucial role in establishing our nation's fundamental freedoms—what I like to call our "human dignities.") The Fourteenth Amendment was added in 1868; it was one of a trio of pivotal amendments that were added shortly after the Civil War. Later, we'll go into more detail about all three.

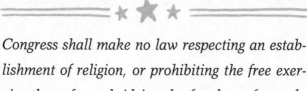

THE FIRST AMENDMENT

Congress shall make no law respecting an establishment of religion, or prohibiting the free exercise thereof; or abridging the freedom of speech, or of the press; or the right of the people peaceably to assemble, and to petition the Government for a redress of grievances.

Look closely at the very beginning of this amendment: "Congress shall make no law." Those five words could not be stronger. They fiercely limit the power of the federal government, and they affirm the supremacy of individual rights. No laws—none whatsoever—can take away the freedoms of religion, speech, and the press. Our basic right to gather peaceably together or to petition for change can never be denied.

King George III was called a tyrant in the Declaration of Independence. The First Amendment is our nation's best defense against the return of any kind of governmental tyranny, especially the kind inflicted on a minority by a majority. In the United States, all people, and all ideas—even unpopular ones—must be treated with respect.

FREEDOM OF RELIGION

We are a nation that honors religion, all religions. Believers of many faiths fought and died in the American Revolution to create a new nation where all could live with dignity. The government of the United States doesn't favor one religion over another. It can't punish anyone for his or her religion.

Thomas Jefferson explained this well, as he explained so many things well.

"No man," he wrote, "shall be compelled to frequent or support religious worship or ministry or shall otherwise suffer on account of his religious opinions or belief, but all men shall be free to profess and by argument to maintain, their opinions in matters of religion."

Those words are inscribed on his memorial in Washington, D.C., which my family visited frequently. My wife and I wanted our children to know these words, and we wanted our guests to be introduced to them.

The Jefferson Memorial is my favorite monument in Washington, D.C. When we took our international guests there, they would read the inscriptions along the walls and on the ceiling and then turn to us in amazement. "America is built on great principles," they would remark.

The First Amendment assures Americans that there will never be an official religion in the United States. Tax dollars collected by Congress can't be used to pay for churches or mosques or temples, or any strictly religious structure. Religious instruction can't be funded with federal money.

"Congress shall make no law respecting an establishment of religion." This is known as the establishment clause of the First Amendment. It draws a line between religious institutions and the government—what is often called the "separation of church and state." But sometimes that line is a little blurry, especially in the schools.

Over the years, many cases about the boundaries between church and state have been argued in the courts, especially the Supreme Court. The highest court

> My Muslim faith is sacred to me, which is why I feel so strongly that church and state must be separate. No political institution has the right to control our spiritual lives. Our most private and personal beliefs belong to us. We can never be truly free if the state tells us how to worship or what to believe.

in the country, generally the last stop in the American legal system, the Supreme Court hears approximately eighty cases each year—usually cases that began in a "lower" court and then were appealed, or reargued, in a "higher" court. The Supreme Court often must tangle with the toughest constitutional questions.

Can a public school begin the day with a voluntary prayer led by a teacher? No, said the court in 1985, when it decided a case that posed that question. Can a public school allow a student religious group to meet after school in the building? Yes, said the court in 2001.

Can public money be used to pay tuition at a religious school? Maybe, the court ruled in 2002—but only under certain circumstances.

The free exercise clause, which directs Congress to pass no laws "prohibiting the free exercise" of religion, works hand in hand with the establishment clause. In a nation where no religion is set above any other, all religions are protected.

Over the years, there have been debates about how to define a religion and exactly what it means to exercise your faith. But the fundamental point is clear: in the United States, you may not be mistreated, penalized, or discriminated against because of your religion.

There are many countries in the world that have an official religion or that privilege people who practice one religion over those who practice another or don't practice any religion at all. Every day, I'm grateful to live in a country that says we are all equal, no matter what we believe. I am Muslim, and I have friends of many different religions and friends who aren't religious. We are all equal in the eyes of our country.

FREEDOM OF SPEECH

When I was growing up in Pakistan, I was told to watch

my words. People who spoke out against the government could be jailed. They could even be killed.

In the United States, we are free to say what we believe. We are free to carry signs that express our opinions or wear caps or T-shirts that promote our views. We can express popular ideas—and unpopular ones, too. Perhaps you've heard someone say this: "I may not agree with what you say, but I will defend your right to say it." That's what freedom of speech is all about.

But it doesn't mean Americans have complete freedom to say *anything* at any time. There are limits. You can't, as the Supreme Court explained nearly a hundred years ago, deliberately cause a panic. You can't threaten violence, or make claims about a product that aren't true, or willfully destroy an innocent person's reputation without risking punishment. Your freedoms aren't meant to be used as weapons.

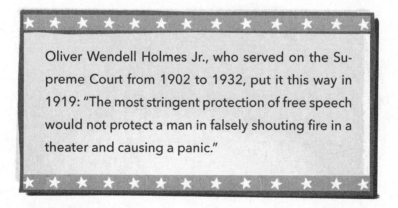

Oliver Wendell Holmes Jr., who served on the Supreme Court from 1902 to 1932, put it this way in 1919: "The most stringent protection of free speech would not protect a man in falsely shouting fire in a theater and causing a panic."

In public schools, students have free speech rights, but school officials are legally allowed to make reasonable rules that might have the effect of punishing certain kinds of speech. You can, for example, be punished for making a rude speech at a school assembly. You can be expelled for cyberbullying.

Freedom of speech is a great privilege, and it's also a great responsibility. We must respect each other's right to speak freely, *especially* when we strongly disagree. Bullies tend to shout down their opponents. Those who love our Constitution listen to other views carefully, consider them seriously, and then add their voices to the debate. Differences of opinion are essential to a healthy society. No one has all the right answers. No one has all the wrong ones. We can't learn from one another unless we know how to listen respectfully to what each person has to say.

Debate is essential to democracy. It's not a reason for division; it's how we move our nation forward. But even when political tensions are high, we are ruled by the authority of laws. That's what guarantees our nation's freedom.

FREEDOM OF THE PRESS

The Constitution created three official branches of government in the United States—legislative, executive, and judicial—and we'll take a closer look at each in later chapters. Unofficially, there is a fourth branch: the press, which is also known as the "media." News that you watch on television or listen to on the radio, posts and videos that appear on the Internet, newspapers, books, magazines, and movies are all part of the media, and they are protected by the First Amendment.

Self-government requires an informed population. You need to know what and whom you're voting for when you go to the polls. You need to know the opinions of the candidates, their background, their character. You need to know what's working well in the government, and what's failing.

When I lived in Pakistan, printing presses were sometimes shut down and even burned when newspapers printed stories the government didn't approve of.

The press can't be under the thumb of the government. It can't be told what stories to publish or what stories to avoid. It has the right—and, many would say, the obligation—to dig, challenge, question, annoy, and exasperate public officials in Washington, D.C., and throughout the country.

The government can't shut down a television station or turn off the Internet or destroy a printing press because the news is bad or critical or because it exposes corrupt, incompetent, or lazy public officials. Free speech requires a free press. Free speech is meaningless if no one can hear it.

The First Amendment doesn't require the press to be fair—or even honest, in some cases—but it insists that the press must be left alone to do its job, which is to report on a wide range of topics and present a broad array of opinion.

Your job as a citizen is to pay attention.

> Berating the media is a common tool of the tyrant. Sometimes this leads to harassment of, and even prison for, journalists. History is full of examples of this tactic, and it was certainly a common trick when I was growing up in Pakistan. That's why it's so important for all of us to defend and support a free press.

FREEDOM TO PEACEABLY ASSEMBLE AND PETITION

These last two rights in the First Amendment aren't as well known as the freedoms of religion, speech, and the press, but they're powerful. They help us stand together. They allow us to combine our voices and amplify our messages.

When you participate in a march or rally or attend any sort of public political event, you are exercising your "right of assembly." All Americans are free to come together and speak out about public policies or public officials without fear of being physically harmed or criminally charged. Large and peaceful crowds can touch the hearts and minds of ordinary citizens and sway the opinions of politicians. During the civil rights struggles of the 1950s and 1960s, massive public gatherings, including the 1963 March on Washington, led by Dr. Martin Luther King Jr., were instrumental in changing voting laws.

In the 1960s, when American civil rights leaders led large protests against racial segregation and unjust voting laws, I was a teenager in Pakistan. Photos of police beatings, snarling dogs, and water cannons aimed at demonstrators saddened and confused me. How could a country like the United States treat its citizens so inhumanely? In time, I was heartened to learn that these injustices could be put right. I discovered the strong American institutions—like Congress and the courts—that could intervene and correct the course of history.

Demonstrators for civil rights during the
1963 March on Washington.

When you have a complaint about a public matter—what the Declaration of Independence calls a "grievance"—you have the right to ask the government to find a solution. You can sign your name to a petition, and you can urge your friends and neighbors to do the same, without fear of punishment. You don't have to rely solely on your elected representatives. You have the authority to tell the government *exactly* what you want.

> When I was growing up in Pakistan, the country was frequently under martial law. That meant that no more than four people could assemble at a time, and everyone was under strict curfew, which was known as Section 144 of the Pakistan Penal Code. Sound trucks would drive through the streets, blaring, "It's now Section 144 time, which will be in place for twelve hours." We wouldn't know when this would happen. But when it did, we were forced inside.

In the world today, there are two kinds of countries: those that support freedom for their citizens and those that suppress it. Billions of people, in dozens of countries, live without the dignities that our Constitution guarantees to every American. To those who live in darkness, America has always been a beacon of hope. The freedoms in our First Amendment are the reason why.

THE FOURTEENTH AMENDMENT

All persons born or naturalized in the United States, and subject to the jurisdiction thereof, are citizens of the United States and of the State wherein they reside. No State shall make or enforce any law which shall abridge the privileges or immunities of citizens of the United States; nor shall any State deprive any person of life, liberty, or property, without due process of law; nor deny to any person within its jurisdiction the equal protection of the laws.

This is the beginning of the Fourteenth Amendment, which became part of the Constitution in 1868, a few years after the end of the Civil War. Later on, you'll find the other four sections of this amendment, but I'm focusing here on this first section because it means so much to me.

> I often become emotional when I read this amendment aloud. The wording is dated, but its meaning is always relevant: everybody is treated equally in this country. All Americans have the same rights in the eyes of our nation, and we are all equally protected by the law.

It's important to me because my wife and I were not born here but rather came to this country as immigrants. It's also important to me because, as a lawyer, I have taken an oath to preserve and protect our nation's laws. But most of all, it's important to me because it represents the goodness and generosity of America.

The Fourteenth Amendment spreads the freedoms of the United States throughout the nation, and it invites the world to share in those liberties.

CITIZENSHIP

If you were born in the United States, you are automatically a citizen of the United States and of the state where you live. It doesn't matter who your parents are or where they were born. All that matters is where *you* were born.

The Fourteenth Amendment was written at a specific time, just three years after the end of the Civil War. It corrected a specific wrong. Before the war, enslaved people had no rights as citizens—even if they had been born on these shores. They couldn't vote. They couldn't own property. In fact, they were routinely treated like property, not like humans. They couldn't even keep their families together if slave owners decided to separate them. Once slavery was abolished after the war, this amendment promised full citizenship to *all* "born or naturalized" Americans— although that promise would not be fulfilled for another century.

My wife and I are among those who are naturalized American citizens. We were born outside the United States, but we became citizens after living in this country for several years, paying taxes, and faithfully fulfilling a number of legal requirements. Our rights as citizens are exactly the same as those of every other American citizen.

As I was about to take the oath of citizenship in 1986, I thought about the privileges being bestowed upon me. I sat there in awe of what was about to happen. I came from a place where I was not able to assemble or protest, where I had to learn to control my tongue and manage my thoughts to avoid being put in jail. Now, I realized, I was about to have the dignities that I was born with as a human being—the dignities Thomas Jefferson wrote about in the Declaration of Independence. In an instant, I went from *not having* to *having*: I walked into that room with no guarantees; I walked out with them. Outside the courthouse, I looked up toward the sky and said a silent prayer of thanks for being able to become a citizen of the United States. It was one of the greatest moments of my life.

The Fourteenth Amendment also promises that every American citizen possesses all the rights and privileges that are found in the United States Constitution. It doesn't matter where you live in America, or what religion you practice, or what color your skin is, or in what country your ancestors were born—you are covered by the same Constitution as every other American citizen.

DUE PROCESS

If you are in the United States, even if you are not a citizen, you have legal rights. The Fourteenth Amendment guarantees this, too. No state can deprive a person— not just a citizen but any *person*—of their "life, liberty, or property, without due process of law."

"Due process" is a broad term, often debated when it comes to specifics. But at its core is a promise: clear and fair legal procedures must be applied to everyone in the same way in the United States. If you are accused of a crime, you have clear and specific rights. Accusations can't be made in secret. Trials can't be held behind closed doors. For the most part, the police and court records of adults must be open to the public.

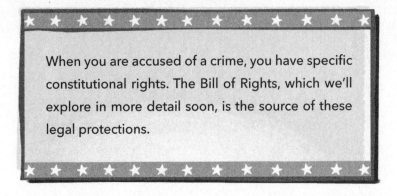

When you are accused of a crime, you have specific constitutional rights. The Bill of Rights, which we'll explore in more detail soon, is the source of these legal protections.

Your property can't be taken by public officials just because they want to take it. Your liberty—your ability to move freely or speak openly—can't be withheld without proper legal proceedings. Your life, which is most precious of all, can't be taken by the government without you having the opportunity to vigorously defend yourself.

Our system of justice is intended to serve *all* in America, not just some.

EQUAL PROTECTION

Every state law must be equally applied to everyone in that state. Your race, your religion, and your gender can't determine how much, or how little, you are covered by a specific law.

This means that election laws can't make voting easier for white Americans than for African Americans. Labor laws can't favor male workers in an industry over female workers in that same industry. Marriage laws can't discriminate based on faith or sexual orientation. A child can't be denied a public education because his or her parents come from another country.

Justice can never be blind—relevant distinctions are important in the law. But in the United States, justice must be impartial. No American should be treated any better, or any worse, than any other American.

I have started with the First and Fourteenth Amendments because they say so much about who we are as Americans and what we value as a nation. But they are just two parts of the Constitution, and there is much more to know about this precious document. Why was

When I was a young law student in Pakistan in the 1970s, it was jokingly said that court rulings can be bought with two bags of cash—one for the corrupt lawyer and the other for the corrupt judge. Not all lawyers and judges are corrupt in authoritative regimes and developing countries, but unfortunately, such practices are common around the world. This results in the suffering of poor citizens who cannot afford the price of "justice."

it written? How was it written? What problems did it solve, and what problems did it create? How did it lay the foundation for our great democracy?

The answers to these questions take us back to Philadelphia in the summer of 1787.

CHAPTER 2

WRITING THE CONSTITUTION

A few dozen men from twelve of the thirteen newly formed original states came to Philadelphia in 1787 to debate the future of the United States. They gathered in the same city, in the same building, and even in the same room, where the Declaration of Independence had been signed eleven years earlier.

Much went right for the United States in its earliest days. It won its war against Great Britain, which at the time was the richest and most powerful empire in the world. Under an agreement known as the Articles of Confederation, it created a new form of government

This is the room in Philadelphia's Independence Hall where the Constitution was written and signed in 1787. The Declaration of Independence was signed in this same room eleven years earlier.

I had the chance to visit this room not long ago. I was tired, and my wife had to drag me there, much as we had dragged our sons to the Washington, D.C., landmarks many years before. But when I stepped inside, I heard the voices of generations past resonating around us. I remember commenting in awe that Pakistan has had constitution after constitution—but Americans continue to live under the same Constitution that was debated and adopted there over two centuries ago.

that, for the most part, allowed each state to govern itself. The national government, small and limited in its powers, was run by members of the Continental Congress, which was made up of representatives from all thirteen states.

But in the years after the Revolution, the newborn nation also experienced its share of growing pains. Some of the problems were so severe that many prominent Americans, including the most prominent American of them all, George Washington, feared that the country was coming apart.

"Our affairs," he noted grimly in 1786, "are drawing rapidly to a crisis."

General Washington had been in Philadelphia for many of the impassioned speeches of the 1770s, but he hadn't planned on returning there, or to public life, once he put away his military uniform. Seven years of fighting was enough. He wanted to enjoy being with his wife and their grandchildren, and living at Mount Vernon, their sprawling plantation along the Potomac River in Virginia. No longer a young man, he wanted to rest.

But he couldn't, not yet, not if he wanted the United States to survive.

Up in the small towns of western and central Massachusetts, tensions were boiling over. Farmers were furious. The taxes on their land kept rising, and their personal incomes kept dropping. Why should they be held responsible for old war debts? Inspired by a Revolutionary War veteran named Daniel Shays, rebels threatened to take over an armory in Springfield, seize its stash of weapons, and arm themselves for a bloody battle against their own state government.

Who had the power to stop this rebellion? The State of Massachusetts? The national government? Who was responsible for this mess—and for similar uprisings? The American Revolution had been over for years. Why hadn't its bills been paid? Who should pay all those bills? The individual states? The Continental Congress?

The new nation had no clear answers to these questions or many others.

More and more, the thirteen states were behaving like thirteen competing countries, not one unified country. Maryland and Virginia were squabbling over their border. New York was taxing ships that sailed from New Jersey. Rhode Island was printing its own paper money, and so were many other states.

The Articles of Confederation, America's first con-

stitution, was written at the beginning of the Revolutionary War. It set the rules for Congress and oversaw
the army. It successfully stitched thirteen former colonies into one loosely connected "firm league of friendship," which stayed friendly (more or less) during the
seven-year fight for freedom. But it established a central government of the United States that had no power
to raise taxes, regulate trade between the states, or
even create a standard form of currency that could be
used in both New York and Rhode Island, or anywhere
else in the United States.

The Articles of Confederation couldn't govern
the growing country indefinitely. The United States
needed a stronger union. It needed a new governing
agreement. It needed a new constitution.

That's what George Washington believed. So did
James Madison, who was also from Virginia.

Madison, a friend and admirer of Thomas Jefferson,
was a small man who must have seemed even smaller
beside the towering figure of Washington. He was one
of the sharpest political thinkers of his generation—
maybe of any generation. Only thirty-six years old,
Madison was the mastermind behind the gathering in
Philadelphia. He had a plan, and his tall fellow Virgin-
ian was at the center of it.

On May 13, 1787, accompanied by three of his slaves, a line of local dignitaries, and a troop of soldiers on horseback, the most famous man in America arrived in Philadelphia. George Washington came as the head of Virginia's delegation—a group of notable men who had been chosen to represent their state at the convention—but everyone knew that he would end up presiding over the entire proceedings.

He was George Washington, after all.

Only Rhode Island declined to send a delegation. The tiniest state was sometimes called Rogue Island by its frustrated neighbors. Independent-minded, it was in the habit of looking out to the sea and turning a blind eye to the rest of the country.

Eventually, fifty-five delegates—many of whom traveled for days or even weeks on horseback or in cramped horse-drawn carriages—made their way to the Pennsylvania State House, known today as Independence Hall, for the Constitutional Convention. They met behind closed doors. Their mouths were supposed to stay shut, too. The delegates vowed to keep the details of their debates secret. Over time, though, word did slip out. James Madison kept a private journal, which he revised over the years. It was published after his death in 1836, and historians have been poring over it ever since.

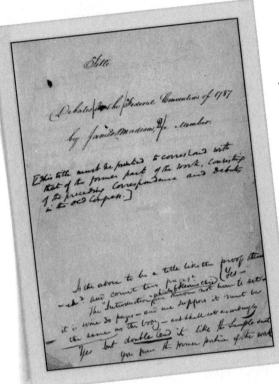

A page from the journal James Madison kept during the Constitutional Convention.

Some delegates stayed in Philadelphia for the whole convention; others came and went. All of them were men. Most were lawyers, and several even had experience drafting the constitutions of their home states. Nearly a third of them were in their twenties or thirties, too young to have been revolutionary leaders back in 1776.

Delegates from the Southern states came well prepared for the Philadelphia summer, with lightweight shirts and linen jackets. New England delegates, on the other hand, outfitted themselves in their best woolen suits. They must have been miserable. Remember, there was no air-conditioning back then, and no electric fans, either. A hot room stayed hot, and tempers probably spiked as the temperature rose. Fortunately, cooler heads prevailed in Independence Hall. The delegates never forgot why they were there.

Everyone at the convention agreed that the Articles of Confederation had problems. But they disagreed about the size of those problems and the best way to fix them.

Yes, said many of the delegates, the Articles of Confederation gives more power to the individual states than to the national government. Yes, they admitted, the Continental Congress is weak. But that's a good thing, they insisted.

Hadn't America just fought a war to free itself from the tyranny of England? A national government with real power would inevitably turn into a national government with too much power. Make a few changes here and there to the Articles of Confederation. That's all this convention needs to do.

No, said the delegation from Virginia, especially Madison. The Articles of Confederation can't be fixed. Let's not even try. The United States needs to be one truly *united* country. A stronger national government will make us all safer and more prosperous.

The Virginians insisted that the United States needed a brand-new constitution. And, as it so happened, Madison, who had thought a great deal about the project, knew what should be in that constitution.

Drawing upon the ideas of the French political philosopher Montesquieu, Madison proposed a federal government that was divided into three branches. The legislative branch, called the Congress, would debate and write the laws. The executive branch, run by the president, would make sure that those laws were carried out. The judicial branch would rule on disputes that arose from those laws.

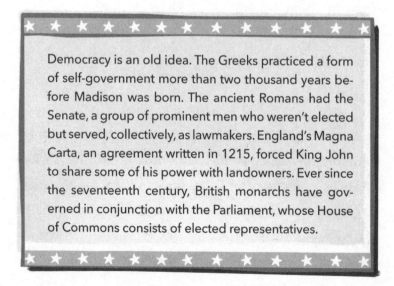

Democracy is an old idea. The Greeks practiced a form of self-government more than two thousand years before Madison was born. The ancient Romans had the Senate, a group of prominent men who weren't elected but served, collectively, as lawmakers. England's Magna Carta, an agreement written in 1215, forced King John to share some of his power with landowners. Ever since the seventeenth century, British monarchs have governed in conjunction with the Parliament, whose House of Commons consists of elected representatives.

CHECKS AND BALANCES IN THE FEDERAL GOVERNMENT

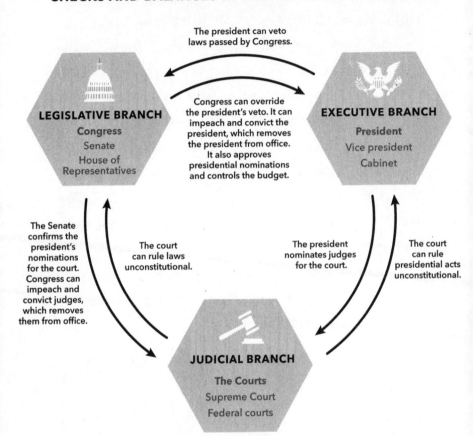

The president can veto laws passed by Congress.

Congress can override the president's veto. It can impeach and convict the president, which removes the president from office. It also approves presidential nominations and controls the budget.

LEGISLATIVE BRANCH
Congress
Senate
House of Representatives

EXECUTIVE BRANCH
President
Vice president
Cabinet

The Senate confirms the president's nominations for the court. Congress can impeach and convict judges, which removes them from office.

The court can rule laws unconstitutional.

The president nominates judges for the court.

The court can rule presidential acts unconstitutional.

JUDICIAL BRANCH
The Courts
Supreme Court
Federal courts

Each branch of the federal government would be powerful, but no branch would be all-powerful. "Checks and balances" were central to Madison's idea. One branch of government could check—that is, limit—the power of another branch. That way, power would be divided among all three branches: there would be balance. No branch would be able to govern without the cooperation of the other two branches. No branch would be able to force its will on the other two branches.

Madison further proposed that the Congress be divided into two parts, or "chambers." One chamber would have many more members than the other. Members of the larger chamber would serve shorter terms than members of the smaller chamber. Voters would directly elect their state's representatives in both chambers. Each state would be allotted seats in both chambers in proportion to its population. This is known as "proportional representation." The more populous the state, the more seats it would hold.

This was called the Virginia Plan.

George Washington, a man of few words, said nothing in support of Madison's proposal, but everyone knew where he stood. He was from Virginia, too.

William Paterson, however, was not from Virginia. He was from New Jersey, a state with a much smaller population than Virginia. He didn't think that the good people of New Jersey should have fewer representatives in Congress than the good people of Virginia. He also thought Congress didn't need to be broken into two chambers. One would do just fine, and each state should get one vote in it.

This was called the New Jersey Plan.

The steamy Philadelphia summer seemed to be getting hotter by the hour as the delegates argued over the two plans. The great scientist and statesman Benjamin Franklin, representing Pennsylvania, thought a morning prayer might soothe the fraying tempers in the hall. Not normally a religious man, the world-famous eighty-one-year-old was one of the handful of delegates who had been there before, in 1776. He was determined to succeed at his last patriotic mission.

In early July, a committee led by a delegate from Connecticut, Roger Sherman, proposed a third way.

It is sometimes called the Connecticut Compromise and is also known as the Great Compromise. It borrowed one idea from the New Jersey Plan and another idea from the Virginia Plan.

The House of Representatives, the larger of the two chambers of Congress, would have its members directly elected by the people of their states. The number of seats held by each state in the House of Representatives would be determined by the size of its population in relation to the population of other states. "Proportional representation" would thus be used in the House.

In the Senate—the smaller chamber—each state

would have the same number of seats. Senators would *not* be directly elected; they would be indirectly elected, chosen by state legislatures whose members had been directly elected. (This method of electing senators lasted for more than a century, until the Seventeenth Amendment was ratified in 1913. Senators are now directly elected by the voters in their state.)

States with more people would have more members in the House of Representatives than states with fewer people. But all states would be equally represented in the Senate.

This was the Great Compromise.

Eventually, this compromise was approved, although not without a lot more arguing. It must have been difficult for Madison to vote for a plan he believed inferior to his own. But he also believed, as did Washington, that there would be no United States—not for very long, anyway—without a new constitution. The two Virginians decided that the only way to get a new constitution was to accept the proposed compromise.

The Great Compromise quieted the conflict between

There were plenty of differences of opinion at the Constitutional Convention, but all the delegates were patriots who loved their country. They believed that America was special.

the larger states and the smaller ones, but another split soon appeared in Philadelphia: the states that relied heavily on the labor of enslaved people versus the states that didn't.

In short, the North versus the South.

1790 POPULATION OF THE UNITED STATES

★ ★ ★

NEW ENGLAND STATES	TOTAL POPULATION	ENSLAVED POPULATION
New Hampshire	141,885	158
Massachusetts	378,787	0
Connecticut	237,946	2,764
Rhode Island	68,825	948

MID-ATLANTIC STATES	TOTAL POPULATION	ENSLAVED POPULATION
New York	340,120	21,324
New Jersey	184,139	11,423
Pennsylvania	434,373	3,737
Delaware	59,092	8,887
Maryland	319,728	103,036

SOUTHERN STATES	TOTAL POPULATION	ENSLAVED POPULATION
Virginia	691,957	287,959
North Carolina	393,751	100,572
South Carolina	249,073	107,094
Georgia	82,548	29,264

If a state's population determined how many seats it would have in the House of Representatives, then the population of each state would have to be carefully counted. But according to what rules? Would *every* person in the state be counted? Or just *some* of the people?

Slave owners insisted that they owned their slaves. Did that mean slaves were property, not people?

The Southern states wanted *all* the people inside their borders to be counted, including the slaves. No one proposed giving slaves the right to vote—that right would be limited to white men who met certain qualifications. But slaves were a significant percentage of the population of Southern states. Nearly half of South Carolina and Virginia were enslaved. Approximately one-third of the people in North Carolina and Georgia were in bondage. Agriculture was the engine of the region's wealth, and the owners of large plantations relied on slave labor to work their fields.

Charles Cotesworth Pinckney, a delegate from South Carolina, put it simply: "South Carolina and Georgia cannot do without slaves." Most members of Virginia's delegation were reliant on enslaved workers as well. The majority of them, including James Madison and George Washington, owned slaves.

If slaves were included in their overall population, the

Southern states would likely have more seats in the House of Representatives than the Northern states. This is why the Northern states insisted that enslaved people *not* be counted. They wanted the North, and not the South, to have the most influence in the new government.

It's important to recognize that there were slaves in the North. They worked in the homes of wealthier families, and also toiled in their fields. But Northern farms tended to be smaller than Southern plantations, and agriculture in the region wasn't dependent on a large labor force, enslaved or free. A movement to ban slavery was gaining ground in New England and spreading to the Mid-Atlantic states. Benjamin Franklin, a former slave owner himself, led an anti-slavery society in Philadelphia. Alexander Hamilton, a delegate from New York, was active in a similar group in Manhattan.

From the writings of the Founding Fathers, we can sense the moral dilemmas they struggled with (as well as those they tried to ignore). On the one hand, they were talking about equal rights; on the other hand, many of them, even George Washington, were going home to legions of slaves. I don't know how they lived with that contradiction. I only know they weren't ready for a revolt on that issue while they were creating the Constitution. Avoiding it all but guaranteed that a catastrophic war was built into the Constitution. However, as we'll see, the solution was made possible through the Constitution's amendment process.

Eventually, a shameful compromise was struck. An enslaved person would count as three-fifths of a person when a state's population was being calculated— slightly more than half a person but less than a whole one. So certain human beings were not counted as full people! Historians have long argued about whether the Constitution could have passed without this horrifying reduction in the value of human life. But no one doubts the grievous harm it did to our nation's principles and values.

Pro-slavery delegates also pushed through a provision that fugitive slaves—enslaved people who ran away from their bondage—must always be returned to bondage if they were found. This meant that a slave who fled Georgia and was later discovered in Massachusetts was legally bound to be returned to Georgia, even though slavery was forbidden in Massachusetts. The laws and customs of the free state wouldn't apply. There would be *no* protection for escaped slaves in this Constitution.

In 1861, the cruel calculations that had been agreed upon in Philadelphia came to a head when the North and the South faced off in a bloody civil war. The Constitution was later amended to right some of those original wrongs, as you'll see in later chapters. But in 1787, and for the next seventy-eight years, they stood.

There was also a serious debate about how much power to give to the president and the executive branch he led. No single person controlled the other two branches of government. The legislative branch consisted of dozens of representatives and senators, and the judicial branch was overseen by a network of judges and court officials. But the executive branch was in the hands of just one person. Was it wise to give so much authority to an individual? Could America's new president turn into a despot, like England's King George III? How would the Constitution ensure that this never happened?

George Washington, as always, kept his thoughts to himself during these discussions, but his presence was impossible to ignore. He was the most admired man in the country, one of the most respected men in the entire world. Without him, America would surely have failed to win its independence. Nearly everyone at the convention, including Washington himself, believed that George Washington would be the first president of the United States—assuming, of course, that there would be such a thing as a president of the United States.

Surely, the most trusted man in America could be trusted to protect his country from tyranny, even his own. He would set the standards that all other presidents would follow.

A five-man committee of "Style and Arrangement" was formed in early September to turn dozens of separate agreements into one unified document. Gouverneur Morris from Pennsylvania became the principal author of the Constitution. He was assisted by Alexander Hamilton from New York, a gifted writer and a speedy one, too. After just four days, the Constitution was written and ready to be voted upon.

George Washington marveled at what was accomplished in Philadelphia. It was "little short of a miracle," he later wrote to the Marquis de Lafayette, a Frenchman who had fought alongside Americans in the Revolutionary War, that "delegates from so many different states . . . should unite in forming a system of national government."

Benjamin Franklin took the floor on the last day of the convention to praise the Constitution and urge all of his fellow delegates, especially those with doubts, to sign it.

[6]

peachments of Officers of the United States; to all cases of Admiralty and Maritime Jurisdiction; to Controversies between two or more States (~~except~~ ~~such as shall regard Territory or jurisdiction~~) between a State and citizens of another State, between citizens of different States, and between a State or the citizens thereof and foreign States, citizens or subjects. In cases of Impeachment, cases affecting Ambassadors, other Public Ministers and Consuls, and those in which a State shall be party, ~~this jurisdiction shall be original.~~ In all the other cases beforementioned ~~it shall be appellate,~~ with such exceptions and under such regulations as the Legislature shall make. The Legislature may assign any part of the jurisdiction abovementioned (except the trial of the President of the United States) in the manner and under the limitations which it shall think proper, to such Inferior Courts as it shall constitute from time to time.

Sect. 4. The trial of all criminal offences (except in cases of impeachments) shall be in the State where they shall be committed; ~~and shall be by jury.~~

Sect. 5. Judgment, in cases of Impeachment, shall not extend further than to removal from office, and disqualification to hold and enjoy any office of honour, trust or profit under the United States. But the party convicted shall nevertheless be liable and subject to indictment, trial, judgment and punishment, according to law.

XII

No State shall coin money; nor grant letters of marque and reprisal; nor enter into any treaty, alliance, or confederation; nor grant any title of nobility.

XIII

No State, without the consent of the Legislature of the United States, shall ~~emit bills of credit, or make any thing but specie tender in payment of debts;~~ lay imposts or duties on imports; nor keep troops or ships of war in time of peace; nor enter into any agreement or compact with another State, or with any foreign power; nor engage in any war, unless it shall be actually invaded by enemies, or the danger of invasion be so imminent, as not to admit of a delay, until the Legislature of the United States can be consulted.

XIIII

The citizens of each State shall be entitled to all privileges and immunities of citizens in the several States.

XIV.

Any person charged with treason, felony, or ~~high misdemeanor~~ in any State, who shall flee from justice, and shall be found in any other State, shall, on demand of the Executive Power of the State from which he fled, be delivered up and removed to the State having jurisdiction of the offence.

XVI.

Full faith shall be given in each State to the acts ~~of the legislatures,~~ and ~~the~~ records and judicial proceedings of ~~the courts and magistrates of~~ every other State.

XVII.

~~New States lawfully constituted or established within the limits of the United States may be admitted, by the Legislature, into this government; but to such admission the consent of two thirds of the Members present in each House shall be necessary.~~ If a new State shall arise within the limits of any of the present States, the consent of the Legislatures of such States shall be also necessary to its admission. ~~If the admission be consented to, the new States shall be admitted on the same terms with the original States. But the Legislature may make conditions with the new States concerning the public debt, which shall be then subsisting.~~

XVII.

[7]

XVIII

agreed —

The United States shall guaranty to each State a Republican form of government; and shall protect each State against ~~foreign~~ invasions, and, on the application of its Legislature, against domestic violence.

XVIIII

agreed —

On the application of the Legislatures of two thirds of the States in the Union, for an amendment of this Constitution, the Legislature of the United States shall call a Convention for that purpose.

XIX.

agreed —

The Members of the Legislatures, and the executive and judicial officers of the United States, and of the several States, shall be bound by oath to support this Constitution.

XXI

agreed —

The ratification of the Conventions of ~~_____~~ States shall be sufficient for organising this Constitution. *between the said States.*

XXII

This Constitution shall be laid before the United States in Congress assembled, ~~_____~~; and it is the opinion of this Convention that it should be afterwards submitted to a Convention chosen in each State, under the recommendation of its Legislature, in order to receive the ratification of such Convention.

XXIII

To introduce this government, it is the opinion of this Convention, that each assenting Convention should notify its assent and ratification to the United States in Congress assembled; that Congress, after receiving the assent and ratification of the Conventions of ~~_____~~ States, should appoint and publish a day, as early as may be, and appoint a place for commencing proceedings under this Constitution; that after such publication, the Legislatures of the several States should elect Members of the Senate, and direct the election of Members of the House of Representatives; and that the Members of the Legislature should meet at the time and place assigned by Congress, and should, as soon as may be, after their meeting, ~~_____~~ proceed to execute this Constitution.

I had a chance to visit the National Archives and see, with my own eyes, a copy of the Constitution with George Washington's markings, or annotations. I've included two pages of it here so you can see it, too. Just imagine, George Washington himself made these notes with his very own quill pen!

"I cannot help expressing a wish," he said, "that every member of the convention, who may still have objections to it, would with me on this occasion doubt a little of his own infallibility, and to make manifest our unanimity, put his name to this instrument."

Set aside your disagreements, the elderly statesman was saying, let go of your ego. For the good of the country, we must act together.

Not everyone heeded Franklin's call for unanimity—three delegates refused, each for his own reasons. But the others who were present took up their pens. On September 17, 1787, after four months of arguing, pondering, and sweating, thirty-nine men from twelve states agreed to a new way of governing their young country.

The doors of that stuffy chamber in Philadelphia were unlocked. The windows were unlatched. Secrecy ended. After four months in a hot room, the Constitution of the United States was ready for the outside world.

But it still had to survive another thirteen rounds of debate, one in each state.

The framers of the Constitution knew the limits of their power. Unless the Constitution was ratified—that is, approved—by a strong majority of the states, it would be a meaningless document. The people needed to understand and support their new government. The

United States could not endure without the consent of its people.

The ratification procedures were clearly spelled out by the framers. First, the Continental Congress, which would be disbanded if the new Constitution was approved, had to consent to sending the agreement on to the individual states. Then each state would convene its own special assembly. The delegates at those assemblies would debate and vote. If nine of those special state assemblies voted yes, then the Constitution would take effect.

The ratification process began smoothly. The Continental Congress promptly agreed to pass along the newly written Constitution to the states, and three states—Delaware, Pennsylvania, and New Jersey—approved it in December 1787. Georgia and Connecticut followed in January 1788. Massachusetts said yes in February, although the debate there was sharp and the vote was a little too close for comfort, 187 to 168. Maryland ratified the Constitution in April 1788; South Carolina, in May.

The future of the Constitution seemed to rest with two very important states: Virginia, home of James Madison and George Washington, and New York, home of Alexander Hamilton. Both states scheduled their special ratification assemblies for the early summer of 1788.

Madison and Hamilton got to work. They knew that Virginians and New Yorkers—like many other Americans, maybe even most other Americans—were largely content with the Articles of Confederation. They knew that many of their friends and colleagues, especially in Virginia, feared that the new Constitution gave too much power to the central government. Hamilton was well aware that many Northerners shared his disgust with the perpetuation of slavery.

They also knew that citizens throughout the country were disappointed that the new Constitution said nothing about individual freedoms.

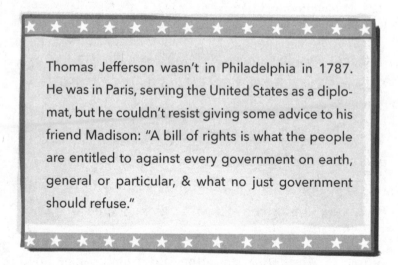

Thomas Jefferson wasn't in Philadelphia in 1787. He was in Paris, serving the United States as a diplomat, but he couldn't resist giving some advice to his friend Madison: "A bill of rights is what the people are entitled to against every government on earth, general or particular, & what no just government should refuse."

Madison understood that these criticisms were coming. Probably better than anyone, he knew the strengths and weaknesses of the new agreement. So almost as soon as there was a Constitution to defend, both he and Hamilton, with a little help from John Jay, another New Yorker, began to defend it.

Beginning in October 1787 and continuing into the summer of 1788, Madison and Hamilton dashed off a series of short political essays, now known as *The Federalist Papers*, that were meant to inform, inspire, and stir up votes for ratification. Similar to opinion pieces that appear on today's editorial pages, these

> I have read *The Federalist Papers*, and I urge you to read them someday. Don't be too discouraged by the language. It's old-fashioned and sometimes hard to follow, but it's worth the effort. These brilliant essays take us right into the minds and hearts of our Founding Fathers.

articles were published in newspapers. Anyone could read them, and many people did. They still do. *The Federalist Papers* continue to shape our understanding of the Constitution.

Virginia opened its ratification assembly on June 2, 1788. Eight states had already voted yes for the

Constitution. Ratification by just one more state would make it the law of the land.

Patrick Henry, a former governor of Virginia and among the most gifted orators of his time, was determined to use all his powers of persuasion to make sure that his home state voted no—emphatically and loudly no. A passionate revolutionary known for his immortal "Give Me Liberty or Give Me Death" speech in 1775, Henry now argued that the agreement would strip away Virginia's right to govern itself and would reduce the individual liberties of Virginians. He didn't trust the checks and balances that Madison had built into the system. He feared that the federal government would become a new kind of tyrant, too large and too powerful to be controlled by ordinary citizens. Many other Virginia delegates shared those fears.

When I first read the Bill of Rights as a young man in Pakistan, I wondered what it would be like to live with these human dignities. Now that I'm a citizen of the United States, I admire the Bill of Rights even more. I know its power. Those of us who are fortunate to live in the United States must always defend and protect the values enshrined in these first ten amendments.

Although no match for Henry as an orator, Madison had a profound grasp of what was actually in the Constitution, especially the procedures for amending it. He assured his fellow delegates that he understood their concerns. He promised them that a "bill of rights," a clear list of individual liberties, would be added to the agreement. He vowed that Virginia and Virginians would be stronger—not weaker—under a new national government.

Madison also had the advantage of having George Washington on his side. Though not in attendance at the Virginia convention, Washington cast a long shadow over the proceedings. It was very hard for Virginians to vote against the wishes of their favorite son.

On June 25, 1787, by a vote of 89 to 79, Virginia ratified the Constitution.

Virginians congratulated themselves on being the ninth state—the deciding state—to ratify the Constitution, but they soon discovered that they were actually the *tenth* state. New Hampshire, as it turned out, was voting while Virginia was still deliberating, and New Hampshire approved the Constitution on June 21, four days before Virginia. But in the days before email, telephones, or even trains, it took several days for word to reach Richmond.

The Constitution was now officially ratified. But the nation still needed to hear from New York. Without its brashest, most vibrant commercial center, the

United States could never compete against the great European powers.

On July 26, 1788, with Alexander Hamilton leading the way, New York voted yes by the slim margin of three votes, 30 to 27.

The United States began anew when New York ratified the Constitution. Although North Carolina and always-stubborn Rhode Island would take a bit longer to make up their minds, the country's direction was set in the summer of 1788. A bold new agreement had been struck with the American people. A new way of governing—devoted to liberty, resolute against tyranny—was launched.

We still sit under the light that was lit during the Constitutional Convention. The framers of our Constitution were hopeful, thoughtful men, and they created a government that honors ideals, hard work, and dignity. We need to remember that— and to hold fast to their spirit as we work together to solve today's challenges.

CHAPTER 3

UNDERSTANDING THE CONSTITUTION

Our Constitution was written to be read and understood by ordinary citizens, not just lawyers, professors, and politicians. And it is still read every day by Americans of all interests and backgrounds, and of all ages, too. You'll find it toward the end of this book. I urge you to read this remarkable document now, and to keep reading it throughout your life.

But we modern readers sometimes need a little help with its language. More than 225 years have passed since the original articles were drafted in Philadelphia.

The English language keeps changing. New words are added, old words fall out of use, and sometimes, over the years, the meaning of a word can even be replaced by its opposite. Scholars of the Constitution spend a lot of time trying to figure out *exactly* what the framers intended.

I'll leave that important work to them.

Instead, here is a version of the United State Constitution that has been rewritten in everyday English. It goes through the documents article by article, section by section, and amendment by amendment.

> I always keep a copy of the Constitution in my breast pocket, and I make a habit of giving copies to as many people as I can. For many years, my wife and I have hosted a dinner for the incoming ROTC class at the University of Virginia. Our beloved son was once a member of this group. We talk about the importance of their service and their defense of the United States Constitution. I'm delighted to say that every soldier walks out of our home with their own copy.

We begin with the Preamble, the introduction, and then move on to the first seven articles, the original core of the Constitution. Amendments make up the final portion of the document. The Bill of Rights, the first ten amendments, was added in 1791. The most recent amendment, the Twenty-Seventh, was passed 201 years later, in 1992.

The more you know about our Constitution, the better you'll see its brilliance and its decency. Every time I read it, my faith in America grows stronger.

THE PREAMBLE

★ ★ ★

We the people of the United States—in order to form a more perfect union among the states, establish justice, ensure peace within our borders, provide a better defense from our enemies, promote our well-being, and secure the blessings of liberty for ourselves and for the future—have created this Constitution, and we are the source of its authority.

When I first read the Preamble as a young law student, it took my breath away. Here was a country that honored justice and fairness. Here was a country that was ruled by laws and guided by principles. Here was a country that knew it wasn't perfect—no place ever is—but had the drive to make itself better, to become *more* perfect. The people had the ultimate power in America, not the military, not the Congress, not even the president. I became a citizen of America because I wanted to be part of its liberties and freedoms. I wanted to pass down these precious gifts to my children and my grandchildren.

ARTICLE I

THE LEGISLATIVE BRANCH OF THE UNITED STATES

★ ★ ★

SECTION 1

AN OVERVIEW OF CONGRESS

Congress is the legislature of the United States, the only branch of the federal government that can write laws. It is divided into two parts, the Senate and the House of Representatives.

SECTION 2

THE HOUSE OF REPRESENTATIVES
OF THE UNITED STATES

Members of the House of Representatives are directly elected by the eligible voters in their states. They serve a two-year term.

Members of the House of Representatives must be at least twenty-five years old, have been citizens of the United States for at least seven years, and, at the time of their elections, live in the state that elected them.

The population of each state determines how many members that state sends to the House of Representatives. It also determines the taxes each state owes the federal government. A state-by-state census, a careful count of its inhabitants, will be taken every ten years. "Free people" will be counted, and so will apprentices and indentured servants, workers who agreed to spend a specific number of years under the control of their employer. Native Americans living on tribal land will not be counted. Enslaved workers will be counted as three-fifths of a person.

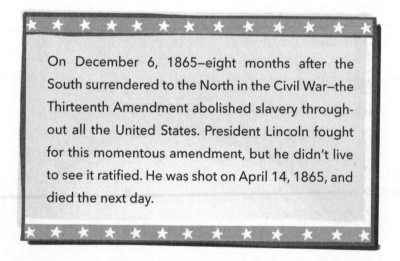

On December 6, 1865—eight months after the South surrendered to the North in the Civil War—the Thirteenth Amendment abolished slavery throughout all the United States. President Lincoln fought for this momentous amendment, but he didn't live to see it ratified. He was shot on April 14, 1865, and died the next day.

When a member of the House of Representatives dies or leaves office between regular elections, that vacancy will be filled by a special election. State governors decide how those elections will be conducted.

Members of the House of Representatives choose their leader, known as the Speaker of the House, and they choose their other officers. The House of Representatives is the only branch of government with the power to impeach—to bring serious legal charges against—the president, the vice president, or other high government officials.

SECTION 3

THE SENATE OF THE UNITED STATES

Each state is represented by two senators, who are elected by their state's legislature. Each senator has one vote in the Senate.

Senators serve a six-year term. The beginning of these terms will be staggered, so that only one-third of the seats in the Senate, approximately, will be up for election at one time. Vacancies that occur between regular elections will be filled by state governors and state legislatures.

Senators must be at least thirty years old by the beginning of their term and have been citizens of the

United States for at least nine years. At the time of their election, they must live in the state that elected them.

The vice president of the United States serves as president of the Senate but has no vote, except to break a tie.

The Senate chooses its officers, including a president *pro tempore,* who presides over the Senate when the vice president of the United States is absent.

If a high government official is impeached—accused of a serious offense—by the House of Representatives, then the trial is held in the Senate, and only in the Senate. Senators must serve at those trials under oath. The chief justice of the United States presides over the trial of a president, who will be convicted if two-thirds of the senators vote for conviction.

People convicted by the Senate will be removed from office and banned from any other public office. They can be further tried for their offenses in regular courts.

SECTION 4
CONGRESSIONAL ELECTIONS
AND CONGRESSIONAL SESSIONS

Congressional elections are overseen by the states,

although Congress may enact laws that alter state procedures. However, Congress does not have the power to change the way senators are elected.

Congress meets at least once a year. New sessions begin on the first Monday of December, unless Congress votes to change that date.

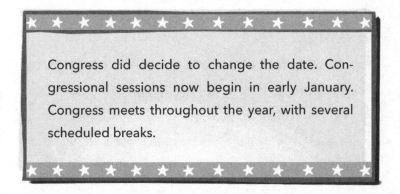

Congress did decide to change the date. Congressional sessions now begin in early January. Congress meets throughout the year, with several scheduled breaks.

SECTION 5

CONGRESSIONAL ORGANIZATION AND RULES

The House of Representatives and the Senate judge the elections and the qualifications of their own members. Half of each chamber's members, a quorum, must be present in order for business to be conducted. Each chamber may punish or expel a member, but only with a two-thirds majority vote. Both the House and the Senate keep a record of their members' votes, provided that one-fifth of their members agree to that practice, and they also keep a record of all their proceedings, except those that must be kept secret. Neither chamber can adjourn for more than three days, or convene at a separate location, without the agreement of the other chamber.

SECTION 6
CONGRESSIONAL PRIVILEGES AND RESTRICTIONS

Members of the House of Representatives and Senate are paid salaries that are established by law and paid for by the United States Treasury. Unless they are accused of a felony, treason, or a breach of the peace, members can't be arrested while they are attending a congressional session or traveling to or from sessions. Their speech in Congress is strictly protected.

Everyone has free speech rights, as the First Amendment makes clear, but the framers made a special point of insisting that members of Congress could never be punished for speaking their minds. Representatives of the people are the voices of the people, and they can't be thrown into jail, tossed out of office, or in any way silenced for expressing their political opinions.

No member of Congress can resign in order to accept a government job that was created during their term in office, or hold a government job whose salary was increased during that period. Serving members of Congress may not hold any other government office.

SECTION 7

PROCEDURES FOR MAKING LAWS

Bills about spending money must originate in the House of Representatives. The Senate may propose amendments to those spending bills, as it can for bills on other issues.

Every bill approved by both the House and the Senate is sent to the president, who can approve it or veto it. If approved, the bill becomes law. If vetoed, it returns to Congress for reconsideration. If both chambers of Congress, each by a two-thirds majority, once again approve the bill, it becomes law. If a bill is presented to the president and the president doesn't act for ten days, excluding Sundays, that bill also becomes law, even though the president didn't sign it. However, if Congress adjourns before the end of that ten-day period, the bill does not become law.

Every order, resolution, or vote that requires the

approval of the House and the Senate, except those concerning adjournment, is also sent to the president. Following the same procedures that apply to bills, these measures can be approved or vetoed by the president, and a two-thirds majority vote in both houses can override a veto.

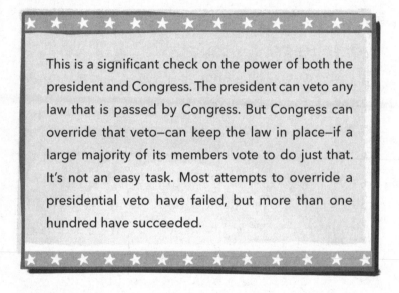

This is a significant check on the power of both the president and Congress. The president can veto any law that is passed by Congress. But Congress can override that veto—can keep the law in place—if a large majority of its members vote to do just that. It's not an easy task. Most attempts to override a presidential veto have failed, but more than one hundred have succeeded.

SECTION 8
POWERS OF CONGRESS

Congress has the power to impose taxes and collect money to pay for the debts, common defense, and well-being of the United States, but all taxes must be uniformly collected throughout the states.

Congress also has the power to:

- borrow money using the credit of the United States

- regulate trade with foreign governments, among the states, and with Native Americans

- establish uniform citizenship requirements and bankruptcy laws for the whole nation

- mint money and set its value, as well as set national standards for the weight and measurement of objects

The United States Mint creates all coins in the country. Every penny you save or spend is produced at one of its four facilities across America.

- punish counterfeiters—criminals who create and distribute fraudulent U.S. currency or securities

- establish the postal service (the post office) and the roads it travels

- promote science and "useful arts" by issuing patents and copyrights (via the U.S. Patent and Trademark Office) that help creators profit from their creations

- establish a federal court system that supports the Supreme Court

- define and punish piracy, felonies on the high seas, and offenses against international law

> Creativity is highly valued in the Constitution. If you have invented a machine, written a book, composed a song, or created something else of enduring value, you have the right to be rewarded for your work. Many of America's greatest fortunes were made by inventors and creative thinkers.

- declare war and make rules concerning captures on land and water

- raise and pay for the army—although Congress can't allocate this money for more than two years at a time

- pay for the navy

- regulate the army and the navy

- call upon state militias—fighting forces that are summoned from time to time—to enforce the nation's laws, put down rebellions, and protect the nation from invasion

- govern state militias when they are acting on behalf of the nation; states, however, appoint militia officers and oversee the training of the militia in accordance with congressional rules

- write laws for the nation's capital, which may not be more than ten square miles in size, and other federal districts

Congress may also enact laws that are "necessary and proper" to enforce these specific powers and all other powers granted to the federal government in the Constitution.

"Necessary and proper" are three little words that have launched a thousand lawsuits. Did they give Congress the power to establish a bank in the nineteenth century? Did they give Congress the power to require health insurance in the twenty-first century? Debates still rage.

SECTION 9
POWERS DENIED TO THE FEDERAL GOVERNMENT

At least until 1808, Congress may not make any laws that limit the importation of slaves into the United States. An import tax of up to ten dollars can be placed on each slave brought into the country.

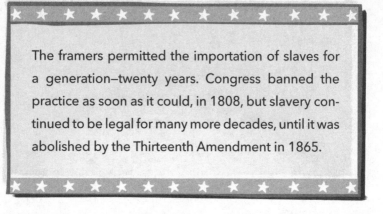

The framers permitted the importation of slaves for a generation—twenty years. Congress banned the practice as soon as it could, in 1808, but slavery continued to be legal for many more decades, until it was abolished by the Thirteenth Amendment in 1865.

A writ of habeas corpus, a legal protection against unjust imprisonment, is required except in times of rebellion or invasion.

A person can't be imprisoned without a fair trial. Laws can't be applied retroactively. If an action was legal when it was taken, it remains legal, even if the laws have since changed.

No individual can be directly taxed by the federal government. All federal taxes must be collected from each state in proportion to the population of that state.

Congress can't tax goods that are sold from one state to another.

The laws in our country look forward, not backward. For example, if your community bans skateboarding in a local park, you can't be fined for having skateboarded there *before* the law was enacted.

The framers were very cautious about taxes. They knew how English taxes had outraged American colonists before the Revolutionary War. But as the country grew larger, so did its needs. What was the best and fairest way to pay America's bills? The Sixteenth Amendment, passed in 1913, allows the federal government to tax the income of individuals.

Congress can't write laws that favor one state's seaports over another's. A ship from one state can't be taxed for using the port of another state.

Federal money may not be spent without congressional approval. All spending must be accounted for and publicly revealed.

In many parts of the world, people are taxed but never know what their money is paying for. Often it's used to enrich the rulers rather than run the country on behalf of the people. This provision in our Constitution directs transparency: the representatives of the American people need to approve all spending. And the people themselves deserve to know how their government is spending money.

Foreign leaders' governments can't enrich officeholders, or other high officials, without the consent of

Congress. No titles of nobility—no dukes, duchesses, earls, princes, and no kings or queens—can ever be granted by the federal government.

SECTION 10
POWERS TO THE STATE THAT ARE DENIED OR LIMITED

States can't make treaties or alliances with foreign governments. They can't authorize privateers. They can't mint coins, print money, or allow debts to be paid by anything other than gold and silver coins. They can't imprison people without trial, and they can't apply laws retroactively. They can't pass laws that invalidate contracts. They can't grant titles of nobility.

States can't tax foreign imports or exports without the consent of Congress, although states are allowed to charge for inspection costs. All taxes collected from foreign imports and exports belong to the federal government and are subject to federal laws.

States can't tax commercial ships for using their ports, form their own armies or navies in a time of peace, or make agreements with other states and foreign governments without the consent of Congress. States can't go to war unless they are being invaded or under immediate threat.

ARTICLE II

THE EXECUTIVE BRANCH OF THE UNITED STATES

★ ★ ★

SECTION 1

ELECTION OF THE PRESIDENT AND VICE PRESIDENT

The president of the United States leads the executive branch and serves a four-year term. The vice president also serves a four-year term.

The president and the vice president are not directly elected by ordinary citizens. They are chosen by electors, who are selected by procedures established by state legislatures. The number of electors in each state is equal to the number of seats that state has in both chambers of Congress. Electors may not be currently serving in Congress or holding a federal office.

★ ★ ★ ★ ★ ★ ★ ★ ★ ★ ★ ★

Our presidential election process is complicated. In some ways, it's actually fifty separate statewide elections (as well as the District of Columbia) for president. We vote for our state's presidential electors, who are members of what's called the

Electoral College. The number of electors in each state is equal to the number of senators and House members in that state. (The District of Columbia has three electors as a result of the Twenty-Third Amendment.) The electors in each state then vote for president and vice president. As a result of this system, it's possible for a candidate to receive fewer popular votes than his or her opponent but still win a majority of votes in the Electoral College and thus become president. This has happened several times in American history, most recently in 2016.

★ ★ ★ ★ ★ ★ ★ ★ ★ ★ ★ ★ ★

Presidential electors meet in their home states and cast two votes each. One of these votes must be for a person who lives outside their state. The person who receives the majority of electoral votes is elected president. The person who receives the second-highest number of electoral votes is elected vice president. The president of the Senate, observed by the House of Representatives and the Senate, certifies these votes. If no candidate receives a majority of the electoral votes, the House of Representatives will choose from among the top five finishers. Each state will be given one vote. If the vote in the House of Representatives is tied for vice president, the Senate will decide that office.

Congress determines the time when electors are appointed and the day they cast their votes. The date is uniform throughout the United States.

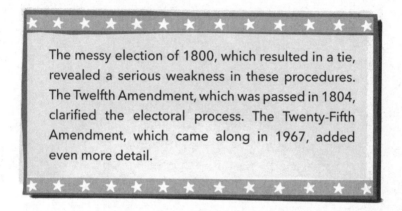

The messy election of 1800, which resulted in a tie, revealed a serious weakness in these procedures. The Twelfth Amendment, which was passed in 1804, clarified the electoral process. The Twenty-Fifth Amendment, which came along in 1967, added even more detail.

The president must be a natural-born citizen of the United States or have been a citizen when the Constitution was adopted. He or she must be at least thirty-five years old and have lived in the country for at least fourteen years.

If the president is removed from office, dies, resigns, or is unable to perform the duties of the office, the vice president becomes the president. Congress may establish further procedures for filling vacancies in the executive branch.

The president receives a salary, which can't be raised or lowered during his or her term of office. The president can't receive any additional income or financial benefits from the federal government or from state governments while in office.

> Presidents take this inaugural oath: "I do solemnly swear (or affirm) that I will faithfully execute the Office of President of the United States, and will to the best of my Ability, preserve, protect and defend the Constitution of the United States."
>
> This last part of the presidential oath doesn't have to apply to just the president! It's up to every one of us to "preserve, protect and defend" our freedoms.
>
> My wife and I attended the commissioning of our son Captain Humayun Khan into the United States Army. We watched as he raised his hand and swore his solemn oath "to support and defend" the Constitution. That moment will always resonate in our memories. How faithful he was to his oath!

SECTION 2

PRESIDENTIAL POWERS

The president is commander in chief of the army and the navy, and of state militias when they are called to serve their nation. The president may request written progress reports from department heads (who are called "cabinet officers") and other high officials in the executive branch. The president may grant reprieves and pardons for all offenses against the United States, except in cases of impeachment.

The president, with the advice and consent of the Senate, has the power to make treaties—agreements about trade or defense—with foreign countries, provided that a two-thirds majority of the Senate approves. The president, with the advice and consent of the Senate, appoints ambassadors and leading diplomats, Supreme Court justices, and other high officers of the United States. Congress may enact laws that give the president, the federal courts, and other high officers the authority to make appointments for less important positions.

The president may temporarily fill vacancies for high offices when the Senate is not in session. These appointments expire at the end of the next Senate session.

SECTION 3

OTHER DUTIES OF THE PRESIDENT

The president from time to time will report on the state of the Union. The president can recommend measures to Congress that are "necessary and expedient." The president may, on extraordinary occasions, convene both the House of Representatives and the Senate, or either of them. If there is a disagreement between the two chambers about when to adjourn—suspend their legislative session—the president will decide the time of adjournment. The president receives foreign ambassadors and ministers. The president makes every effort to ensure that federal laws are properly executed. The president commissions—grants official authority to—all officers of the United States.

SECTION 4
IMPEACHMENT AND REMOVAL FROM OFFICE

The president, vice president, and all other civil officers of the United States will be removed from office if they are charged and found guilty of treason, bribery, or other "high Crimes and Misdemeanors."

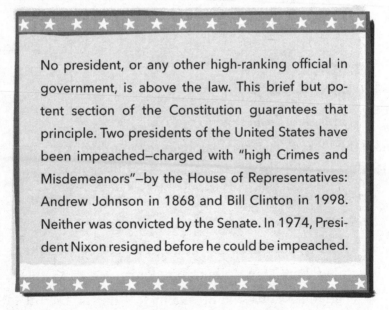

No president, or any other high-ranking official in government, is above the law. This brief but potent section of the Constitution guarantees that principle. Two presidents of the United States have been impeached—charged with "high Crimes and Misdemeanors"—by the House of Representatives: Andrew Johnson in 1868 and Bill Clinton in 1998. Neither was convicted by the Senate. In 1974, President Nixon resigned before he could be impeached.

ARTICLE III

THE JUDICIAL BRANCH OF THE UNITED STATES

★ ★ ★

> To me, this article highlights the primacy of the rule of law in a democracy. The entire judicial system, with the Supreme Court at its head, exists to serve this inspiring concept—of a peaceful nation governed by consistent laws and a court that impartially oversees those laws.

SECTION 1

AN OVERVIEW OF FEDERAL COURTS

The Supreme Court is the highest court in the United States. Congress may also create a system of lower federal courts. Federal judges do not have set terms and may serve as long as they exhibit good behavior. Federal judges are paid a salary, which may not be reduced while they serve.

The Supreme Court in Washington, D.C.

Each branch of government has its own distinctive building. The White House is home to the president, the head of the executive branch. The Capitol houses the legislative branch—the Senate and the House of Representatives. The Supreme Court Building belongs to the most powerful court in the judicial branch. The three buildings form a triangle, and the Supreme Court Building occupies the highest ground. This pleases me as a lawyer and an advocate for justice.

SECTION 2

AUTHORITY OF THE SUPREME COURT
AND OTHER FEDERAL COURTS

Federal courts hear cases that involve the Constitution, federal laws, and international treaties. They hear cases that concern ambassadors and other foreign emissaries. They rule on disputes at sea. They judge cases in which the United States is a party. They judge cases between two or more states, between a state and a citizen of another state, and between citizens of two different states. They judge land disputes among states, and land or other disputes in the United States that involve foreign governments or people.

> Lawyers generally refer to the federal courts as Article III courts, and we call the judges who preside over them Article III judges. This is because the federal judicial system was created under Article III of our Constitution.

Cases concerning ambassadors and foreign emissaries originate in the Supreme Court. So do cases in which a state is a party. But most federal cases are argued in an appellate court—a court that hears cases that have been tried in lower courts and then been "appealed" to a higher court for another decision.

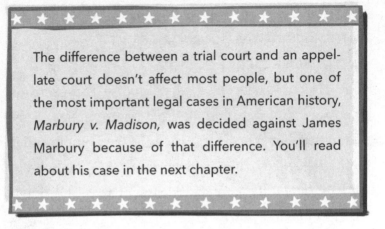

The difference between a trial court and an appellate court doesn't affect most people, but one of the most important legal cases in American history, *Marbury v. Madison*, was decided against James Marbury because of that difference. You'll read about his case in the next chapter.

Anyone who is charged with a crime against the federal government—with the exception of cases of impeachment—has the right to trial by a jury. Trials are held in the state where the crime was alleged to have been committed. Congress can legislate trial procedures for crimes that are not committed within one state.

SECTION 3
TREASON

Treason is a strictly defined crime. Americans who form armies and fight against the United States, or give aid and comfort to foreign enemies, can be found guilty of treason. A conviction for treason requires that two witnesses testify against the accused traitor or that the accused traitor confesses in open court.

Congress determines the punishment for treason. That punishment, however, is to be given only to the convicted traitor, not to his or her family. Property that belonged to a convicted traitor may not be seized by the government after his or her death.

> The framers of the Constitution had no sympathy for traitors, but it's important to remember that treason is not about criticism. Arming America's enemies, divulging secrets, joining an enemy army—these are acts of treason. Criticizing public officials or protesting public policies is not treason. It's exercising your First Amendment rights.

ARTICLE IV

RELATIONSHIPS BETWEEN THE STATES

★ ★ ★

SECTION 1
RESPECTING STATE LAWS AND JUDGMENTS

Each state must respect the laws, records, and judgments of every other state. Congress establishes the procedures for proving the authenticity of those judicial rulings and public records.

SECTION 2
DUTIES OF THE STATES TO EACH OTHER

A citizen in one state is a citizen of all the states. All the rights and privileges given to the citizen of one state must also be given to the citizens of every other state.

> This provision asserts that the states have been united into one nation. All Americans are entitled to equal treatment throughout the country, no matter where they come from or where they're going.

A fugitive from justice from one state who is found in another state must be returned to the original state if its governor orders his or her return.

Slaves who flee bondage, and are found anywhere in the United States, must be returned to bondage. Indentured servants who abandon their employer without completing their term of service must be returned to their employer.

This loathsome requirement ended when the Thirteenth Amendment abolished slavery in 1865.

SECTION 3
NEW STATES AND TERRITORIES

Congress may admit new states to the nation. However, no new state can be formed within a state, or from the parts of two or more states, without the approval of the legislatures of those states and of Congress.

Congress governs federal territory and property, such as national parks and military bases.

SECTION 4
FEDERAL GUARANTEES TO THE STATES

The United States guarantees that all states will have a representative form of government. The United States guarantees to protect states that are invaded by foreign forces. Upon the request of a governor or a state legislature, the United States may also protect states that are threatened from violent forces within the state.

ARTICLE V

AMENDING THE CONSTITUTION

★ ★ ★

An amendment to the Constitution can be proposed by Congress after a two-thirds majority vote in both the House of Representatives and the Senate, or it can be proposed in a constitutional convention called by two-thirds of the state legislatures. The proposed amendment must then be approved by three-quarters of the states, either by vote of their legislatures or by special conventions. No amendment may be made to this Constitution about the importation of slaves (see Article I, Section 9) until 1808. No amendment can ever reduce, without the consent of the state, the number of Senate seats available to a state.

The amendment process is our Constitution's greatest strength. It allows our nation to adjust to changing circumstances but also hold on to enduring values.

It's not easy to amend the Constitution. The procedure is laborious, but the rules are clear and the path is available to those who are determined to bring about change.

The Preamble speaks of a "more perfect Union," not a perfect Union. The Founding Fathers knew there would always be room to make our nation better. The amendment process, thoughtfully and carefully exercised, helps us do this. That's what makes the Constitution a living document.

ARTICLE VI

OBLIGATIONS AND LOYALTIES

★ ★ ★

All the debts and financial obligations that the United States agreed to before this Constitution will continue to be honored.

The Constitution, the laws of the United States, and all treaties are the highest law in the land. All judges in every state must abide by this Constitution, regardless of their state's constitution or its laws.

All members of the House of Representatives, Senate, and state legislatures, and all judges and executive officials, in the federal government or the state governments, must take an oath (or make an affirmation) to defend this Constitution.

No religious test will ever be required for public officials.

My eyes welled up with tears as I waited in the courthouse to take my oath as a new American lawyer. It was overwhelming for me to realize that I now had the authority to offer legal opinions and to defend others.

ARTICLE VII

RATIFICATION PROCEDURES

★ ★ ★

Each state will hold a special constitutional convention. This Constitution will go into effect after it is approved by nine states.

AMENDMENTS TO THE CONSTITUTION

* ★ *

The first ten amendments to the Constitution are called the Bill of Rights because they lay out the fundamental rights and freedoms enjoyed by all Americans. These are the individual liberties—the human dignities—that Patrick Henry of Virginia, along with so many others who debated the merits of the Constitution, insisted upon adding to the document. Almost as soon as the first Congress was convened in 1789, James Madison started working on a bill of rights. Two years later, these ten amendments were ratified.

FIRST AMENDMENT
FREEDOM OF RELIGION, SPEECH, THE PRESS, AND ASSEMBLY (1791)

Congress may not make laws that establish an official religion in the United States or prevent believers from freely practicing their religion. Congress may not limit free speech or a free press. Congress must allow people the right to gather publicly in peaceful protest against their government and to petition their government to address their complaints or concerns.

SECOND AMENDMENT
RIGHT TO FIREARMS (1791)

Because militias are necessary to protect the nation, people have a fundamental right to keep and use firearms.

THIRD AMENDMENT
HOUSING OF SOLDIERS (1791)

In times of peace, citizens can't be forced to house soldiers. In times of war, laws will regulate when and how citizens must provide military housing.

FOURTH AMENDMENT
PRIVACY RIGHTS FOR PEOPLE AND PROPERTY (1791)

People and property can't be searched or taken for no reason. A search warrant, which specifies the reason for the search and the object of that search, must be provided by a judge. Police officers or other officials are required to take an oath of honesty when they request a search warrant.

Where I grew up, "search and seizure" was a privilege of authority. The police could knock at any time on any door and arrest someone. Why? For any reason—such as claiming that the person had participated in a demonstration. That's the way it is in authoritarian regimes. When I first read this part of the Constitution, I wondered, Did we in Pakistan get it wrong? Did we forget that privacy and property are *not* privileges of authority? I never take these rights for granted.

FIFTH AMENDMENT
RIGHTS OF THE ACCUSED (1791)

No one will be accused of a serious federal crime unless a grand jury—a jury of ordinary citizens—decides that the government has sufficient evidence of the crime. However, accused members of the military or the militia, in times of war or public danger, do not have this protection. No person can be tried twice for the same crime. No one can be forced to testify against himself or herself. The government can't take a person's life, liberty, or property without following established legal procedures. Private property can't be taken for public use unless the owner is fairly compensated.

SIXTH AMENDMENT
RIGHT TO A FAIR TRIAL (1791)

Everyone accused of a crime has the right to a speedy and public trial, which is decided by an open-minded jury of citizens who live in the district where the offense was alleged to have been committed. The accused must be told what crime they are accused of and what evidence supports that accusation. They have a right to present witnesses who will defend them against those charges. They have a right to an attorney.

As an American and a lawyer, I take great pride in the fact that our Constitution guarantees a fair trial. In many other nations, only the wealthy have access to justice. Here, all citizens have rights, even when accused of committing a crime. But too many Americans, especially the poor and members of minority groups, feel unprotected by our judicial system. It's up to all of us to ensure that our nation honors its commitment to fairness and equal treatment for all.

SEVENTH AMENDMENT
CIVIL TRIALS (1791)

In civil cases—those not about criminal matters—everyone has a right to a trial by jury if the amount at stake in a dispute is more than twenty dollars. All cases must be tried in courts that follow standard legal procedures.

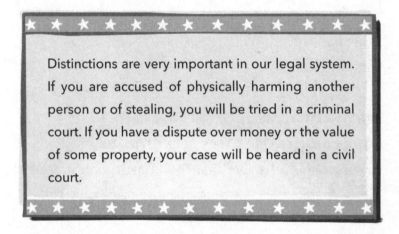

Distinctions are very important in our legal system. If you are accused of physically harming another person or of stealing, you will be tried in a criminal court. If you have a dispute over money or the value of some property, your case will be heard in a civil court.

EIGHTH AMENDMENT
APPROPRIATE PENALTIES (1791)

Courts can't impose excessive bail—a temporary payment that permits an accused citizen to avoid jail while awaiting trial. Nor can courts impose excessive fines. Cruel and unusual punishments can't be inflicted by the courts.

"Cruel and unusual punishment" is another of those constitutional phrases that spark heated debate. Is it cruel and unusual for a state to impose the death penalty on a convicted murderer? Many Americans say yes. Many say no. Each generation struggles with the practical meaning of "cruel and unusual punishment," and our standards continue to evolve.

NINTH AMENDMENT
OTHER RIGHTS OF STATES AND CITIZENS (1791)

No one should believe that the Constitution presents *all* rights. American citizens also have rights that don't appear in this document.

TENTH AMENDMENT
STATE AND INDIVIDUAL POWERS (1791)

All powers that are not granted to the federal government in this Constitution, or not denied to the states, are held by the states or by the people themselves.

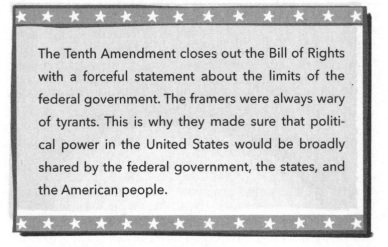

The Tenth Amendment closes out the Bill of Rights with a forceful statement about the limits of the federal government. The framers were always wary of tyrants. This is why they made sure that political power in the United States would be broadly shared by the federal government, the states, and the American people.

ELEVENTH AMENDMENT
FEDERAL COURT LIMITS (1795)

State governments can't be sued in federal court by residents of other states or citizens of other nations.

TWELFTH AMENDMENT
ELECTORAL COLLEGE CHANGES (1804)

Procedures for Presidential and Vice Presidential Elections

The president and the vice president of the United States are chosen by electors, who meet in their home states (see Article II, Section 1). Each elector votes specifically for a president and specifically for a vice president, one of whom must live outside the elector's state. These votes are counted and certified by each state, and then the results are delivered to the president of the Senate. In full view of the House of Representatives and the Senate, the president of the Senate counts the votes from each state. Whoever wins the majority of the electoral votes for president is elected president. Whoever wins the majority of the electoral votes for vice president is elected vice president.

If no candidate wins a majority of the electoral votes for president, the House of Representatives has the authority to choose the president from among the top three finishers. Each state will be allotted one vote for president, and at least two-thirds of the states must be represented at the vote. Whoever wins the majority of the votes cast in the House will be elected president. If no president is chosen by January 20 in the year following the election, the vice president shall serve as president.

★ ★ ★ ★ ★ ★ ★ ★ ★ ★ ★ ★ ★

Sometimes a bad experience can be the best teacher. The election of 1800 resulted in a tie in the Electoral College between two members of the same political party, Thomas Jefferson and Aaron Burr. This amendment, which required electors to make separate votes for president and vice president, was designed to prevent that from ever happening again. But it's still mathematically possible for candidates from opposing parties to be tied in the Electoral College.

★ ★ ★ ★ ★ ★ ★ ★ ★ ★ ★ ★ ★ ★

Vice Presidential Elections in the Senate

Whoever wins the majority of the electoral votes for vice president is elected vice president. However, if no vice presidential candidate has that majority, the Senate chooses the winner from between the top two finishers. At least two-thirds of the Senate must participate in the vote, and whoever wins the majority of the Senate's votes is elected vice president. The vice president must also be constitutionally eligible to be president.

THIRTEENTH AMENDMENT
ABOLITION OF SLAVERY (1865)

Slavery is forbidden in the United States and any place

under its legal control. Indentured service—being forced to work without pay—is also forbidden, except as punishment for convicted criminals.

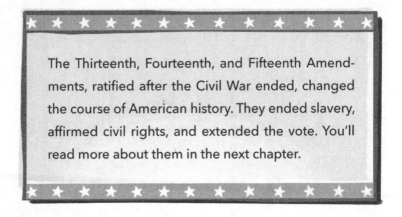

The Thirteenth, Fourteenth, and Fifteenth Amendments, ratified after the Civil War ended, changed the course of American history. They ended slavery, affirmed civil rights, and extended the vote. You'll read more about them in the next chapter.

FOURTEENTH AMENDMENT
CIVIL RIGHTS (1868)

Everyone who was born in the United States, or has become naturalized through the nation's laws, is a citizen of the United States and of the state in which he or she lives. No state can make or enforce laws that restrict the rights of citizenship. No state can deprive a person of life, liberty, or property without following established legal procedures. All people in a state must be treated equally by the laws of that state.

States that restrict voting rights for eligible male voters will lose members in the House of Representatives.

Anyone who took an oath to defend the Constitution of the United States and then fought against the United States in a civil war, or other insurrection, is ineligible to hold high office unless approved by a two-thirds majority vote in both chambers of Congress.

All debts incurred by the United States to protect itself from rebellion, including the pensions of soldiers, will be honored. The United States, and all of its states, will not pay any debts, including those associated with slavery, incurred by anyone engaged in rebellion.

Congress may enact laws to enforce these provisions.

> We've already discussed the Fourteenth Amendment in detail in chapter 1. You can go back and revisit this important part of our Constitution there.

FIFTEENTH AMENDMENT
VOTING RIGHTS (1870)

The right to vote can't be denied because of race or color, or because the voter was previously a slave.

Congress may enact laws to enforce this provision.

SIXTEENTH AMENDMENT
INCOME TAXES (1913)

Congress has the right to impose and collect income

taxes. It can collect these taxes without regard to the size of each state's population.

One of the very first steps on the path to becoming a citizen is paying income taxes—giving a portion of the money you earn to the government to help fund services our country relies on. During our application process, my wife and I were required to prove that we had been paying federal income taxes for years. All who wish to become American citizens must meet this requirement. We did so with pride. Thirty years later, we are still proud to pay our taxes—federal, state, and local. Our taxes help pay for the schools we learn in, the military that protects us, our police officers and firefighters, our judges and courts, the roads we drive on, our playgrounds and parks, the cleaning of our streets— for what the Preamble to the Constitution calls the "general Welfare" of our nation.

Every year you can see where your family's federal taxes go. It's on a chart that appears on the Internal Revenue Service's tax forms.

Major Categories of Federal Income and Outlays for Fiscal Year 2015

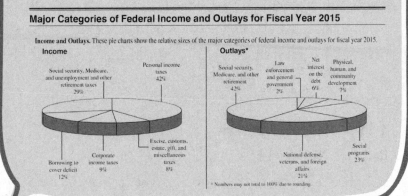

Income and Outlays. These pie charts show the relative sizes of the major categories of federal income and outlays for fiscal year 2015.

Income

- Social security, Medicare, and unemployment and other retirement taxes 29%
- Personal income taxes 42%
- Excise, customs, estate, gift, and miscellaneous taxes 8%
- Corporate income taxes 9%
- Borrowing to cover deficit 12%

Outlays*

- Social security, Medicare, and other retirement 42%
- Law enforcement and general government 2%
- Net interest on the debt 6%
- Physical, human, and community development 7%
- Social programs 23%
- National defense, veterans, and foreign affairs 21%

* Numbers may not total to 100% due to rounding.

SEVENTEENTH AMENDMENT
ELECTION OF SENATORS (1913)

All senators will be directly elected by the citizens of their state.

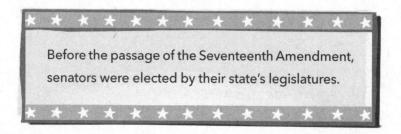

Before the passage of the Seventeenth Amendment, senators were elected by their state's legislatures.

When there is a vacancy in the Senate, the governor of the affected state can call for a new election. A governor can also appoint a temporary replacement if given the authority by the state's legislature.

Senators who were elected before this amendment was enacted are not affected by it until the end of their term.

EIGHTEENTH AMENDMENT
PROHIBITION OF ALCOHOL (1919)

Intoxicating liquors, such as beer and wine, will be forbidden in the United States. They may not be manufactured, transported, or sold. This amendment will take effect one year after its ratification.

Congress and the states may enact laws to enforce this provision.

This amendment will not go into effect unless it is ratified by the states within seven years.

NINETEENTH AMENDMENT
WOMEN'S SUFFRAGE (1920)

No citizen can be denied the right to vote because of her gender. Congress may enact laws to enforce this provision.

My wife and I were amazed when we discovered that this amendment wasn't passed until 1920. Imagine, for nearly 150 years the women in this great democracy did not have the right to vote! Women in many other countries had won that fundamental right much earlier. And why is it still so rare for an American woman to hold a high elective office? We believe there is much work to be done to give all the women in this country an equal opportunity to live with full dignity.

TWENTIETH AMENDMENT
TERMS OF OFFICE (1933)

After an election, the terms of the sitting president and vice president end at noon on January 20, when the terms of the next president and vice president begin. Similarly, members of the House of Representatives and the Senate end and begin their terms on January 3.

Congress meets at least once a year, beginning on January 3, unless it votes for another date.

If the president-elect dies before taking office, the vice president–elect becomes president. If a president has not been chosen before the start of a new presidential term, or if the president-elect has failed to qualify for the office, the vice president–elect serves as president until a new president is chosen. If both the president-elect and the vice president–elect fail to qualify for the office, Congress may lawfully declare an acting president, who serves until a president-elect or vice president–elect is found to be qualified.

If the House of Representatives elects a president who dies before his or her term begins, or if the Senate elects a vice president who dies before his or her term begins, Congress may enact new laws for filling those offices.

The first two sections of this amendment, after its ratification, take effect on October 15.

This amendment will not go into effect unless it is ratified by the states within seven years.

TWENTY-FIRST AMENDMENT
REPEAL OF PROHIBITION (1933)

The Eighteenth Amendment to the Constitution, which prohibits intoxicating liquors throughout the United States, is repealed.

States, territories, or any other area under the control of the federal government may still pass laws that prevent the sale and transportation of alcohol.

This amendment will not go into effect unless it is ratified by the states within seven years.

★ ★ ★ ★ ★ ★ ★ ★ ★ ★ ★ ★ ★

Supporters of the Eighteenth Amendment believed that America would be safer, healthier, and happier without alcohol. But Americans didn't stop drinking just because alcohol was illegal.

Liquor was still widely available—but now it was sold by criminals, many of them organized into gangs, and it cost more than ever. Thirteen years after the prohibition of alcohol began, it ended with the passage of this amendment. The Eighteenth Amendment is, so far, the only one ever to be repealed.

TWENTY-SECOND AMENDMENT
PRESIDENTIAL TERM LIMITS (1951)

A president can be elected to only two terms in office. If a vice president, or some other official, becomes president and serves for more than two years in that office, then he or she may run for just one more term.

This amendment applies to future presidents, not the current one.

This amendment will not go into effect unless it is ratified by the states within seven years.

Up until 1951, there was no limit on the number of terms a president could serve. George Washington had stopped at two, so that became the tradition until Franklin Delano Roosevelt decided to run for a third term—and then a fourth. This amendment turned Washington's tradition into law. Two terms is now the legal limit for every president.

Our Founding Father
George Washington.

TWENTY-THIRD AMENDMENT
PRESIDENTIAL ELECTIONS IN THE DISTRICT
OF COLUMBIA (1961)

The District of Columbia, even though it is not a state, will be allocated presidential and vice presidential electors in proportion to its population, but never less than three. These electors will meet in the District

The framers decided that the United States needed a new capital city that was independent—that is, not under the control of any one state. What they couldn't foresee was how large the population of the District of Columbia would grow. Over time it became clear that the residents of Washington, D.C., deserved a way to vote for president.

of Columbia and follow the procedures found in the Twelfth Amendment.

Congress may enact laws to enforce this amendment.

TWENTY-FOURTH AMENDMENT
ABOLISHING POLL TAXES (1964)

No state can require a citizen to pay a tax in order to vote for president, vice president, senator, or a member of the House of Representatives.

Congress has the power to enact laws to enforce this amendment.

By the time the Twenty-Fourth Amendment was written, African American males (and later females) had long had the right to vote. But in many places in the South, it was all but impossible for them to exercise that right. Southern blacks were often given unpassable literacy tests or forced to pay a poll tax—a fee for voting. The civil rights protests and marches of the 1950s and 1960s fueled a number of important changes in American society, including the Voting Rights Act of 1965, which outlawed literacy tests, and this amendment, which abolished poll taxes.

TWENTY-FIFTH AMENDMENT
PRESIDENTIAL SUCCESSION (1967)

If a president is removed from office, dies, or resigns, the vice president becomes president.

If there is no sitting vice president, the president may nominate one, who must be approved by a majority vote in both the House of Representatives and the Senate.

If a president feels unable to perform his or her duties, he or she must inform, in writing, the president *pro tempore* of the Senate and the Speaker of the House. The vice president serves as president until the president declares, also in writing, that he or she feels fit enough to return to the presidency.

If the vice president and a majority of the cabinet inform the president *pro tempore* of the Senate and the Speaker of the House that the president is unable to perform the duties of the office, the vice president becomes acting president.

When the president declares his or her fitness to return to the office, he or she once again has all presidential powers, *unless,* within four days, the vice president and a majority of the cabinet inform, in writing, the president *pro tempore* of the Senate and the Speaker of the House that they don't believe the president is ready to serve. Congress must meet within forty-eight hours to discuss the situation and must act within twenty-one days. If a two-thirds majority of both chambers agrees that the president is unable to perform his or her duties, the vice president becomes acting president. If that majority is not reached, the president continues in office.

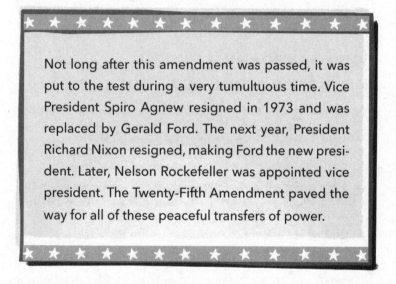

Not long after this amendment was passed, it was put to the test during a very tumultuous time. Vice President Spiro Agnew resigned in 1973 and was replaced by Gerald Ford. The next year, President Richard Nixon resigned, making Ford the new president. Later, Nelson Rockefeller was appointed vice president. The Twenty-Fifth Amendment paved the way for all of these peaceful transfers of power.

TWENTY-SIXTH AMENDMENT
LOWERING THE VOTING AGE (1971)
Citizens of the United States who are eighteen years old or older have the right to vote.

Congress has the right to enact laws to enforce this amendment.

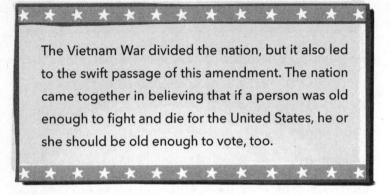

The Vietnam War divided the nation, but it also led to the swift passage of this amendment. The nation came together in believing that if a person was old enough to fight and die for the United States, he or she should be old enough to vote, too.

TWENTY-SEVENTH AMENDMENT

CONGRESSIONAL PAY RAISES (1992)

When Congress votes itself a pay raise, the increase can't take effect until after the next election.

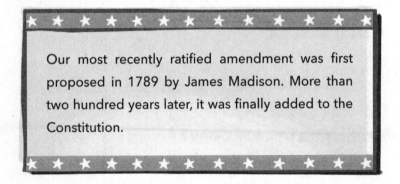

Our most recently ratified amendment was first proposed in 1789 by James Madison. More than two hundred years later, it was finally added to the Constitution.

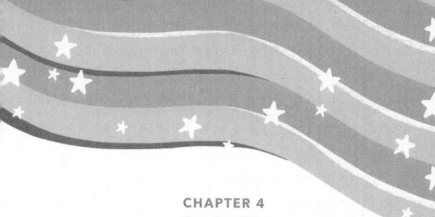

CHAPTER 4

PERFECTING THE CONSTITUTION

In 1803, about a decade after the Bill of Rights was ratified, President Thomas Jefferson mused about the Constitution. "Let us go on then perfecting it," he suggested to a younger colleague, "by adding, by way of amendment to the Constitution, those powers which time and trial show are still wanting."

It would take time and experience, Jefferson believed, for Americans to fully grasp their Constitution. Only by living with it would we appreciate its strengths and learn how to correct its weaknesses. Back in 1787, the framers in Philadelphia had established the legal principles and ideals that guide our country, but the day-to-day task of governing has always been messy and complicated. People of good faith have always disagreed about how to put political beliefs into action, and we continue to do so today.

What happens when disputes arise over the meaning of the Constitution? What happens when a future generation decides that the framers of the Constitution were wrong? What happens when new situations arise that the framers could never have imagined?

For nearly 250 years, our nation has usually responded to these challenges calmly and peacefully, but not always. We argue about the Constitution so passionately because we believe in it so deeply.

Here we'll take a closer look at several amendments—efforts to "perfect" the Constitution, to use Jefferson's term. We'll also explore how the Constitution has been interpreted—and sometimes reinterpreted—over the years.

THE BILL OF RIGHTS

★ ★ ★

RATIFIED IN 1791

Even before Benjamin Franklin reminded them of their fallibility, the framers of the Constitution knew that their work wasn't faultless. They knew improvements would be required. They expected changes to be made. They even created a road map for making those changes.

Article V is one of the shortest parts of the Constitution, but it's among the most powerful. It spells out the procedures for proposing and passing amendments, and it insists that amendments "shall be valid to all Intents and Purposes, as Part of this Constitution."

In other words, amendments are just as important as every section in the original document. That was always the intention of the framers. In fact, even before the Constitution was ratified, amendments to it were being strenuously debated.

At the state ratification conventions, a number of

delegates—most famously, Patrick Henry of Virginia—complained that the document that came out of Philadelphia said nothing about individual rights. Where were the legal protections for ordinary Americans? Where were the guarantees for freedom of speech and freedom of assembly? What about property rights? Should Americans worry that the new government could take their possessions?

The proposed Constitution was too quiet about these fundamental matters.

James Madison and Alexander Hamilton, probably the two most outspoken defenders of the Constitution, initially argued that it didn't need a list of individual rights. All those rights and protections are already in there, they said. Not explicitly, but implicitly. There was no cause for worry.

But the critics *did* worry. They wanted specifics, and so did Thomas Jefferson. He thought the Constitution needed "a declaration of rights," he explained to a friend, "one which shall stipulate freedom of religion, freedom of the press, freedom of commerce against monopolies, trial by juries in all cases, no suspensions of the habeas corpus, no standing armies."

Eventually, Madison agreed. A bill of rights, a clear and easy-to-understand list of fundamental rights, he realized, would give Americans greater faith in the new Constitution. It would help people know where they stood. It would assure Americans that their cherished personal freedoms would not be stripped away by the new government.

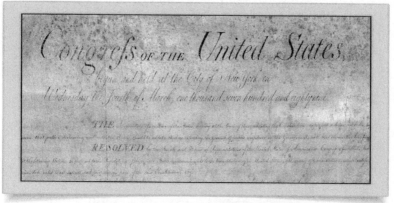

A portion of the original Bill of Rights.

The politically savvy Madison knew that without the promise of a bill of rights, Virginia would probably vote against ratification. And he also knew that without the support of Virginia, the Constitution would be fatally weakened, and so would the United States.

The first ten amendments to the Constitution, the Bill of Rights, were enacted in 1791, and they have served as the cornerstones of American liberty ever since. Madison led the ratification effort, just as he'd vowed he would.

The freedoms of the First Amendment—religion, speech, the press, assembly, and the right to petition— are cherished by me, as I discussed in the first chapter. They are fundamental to our legal and moral values as Americans.

The Second Amendment, the right to own and use guns, is one of the most controversial passages in the Constitution. Unlike most other amendments, it begins with an observation: "A well regulated Militia, being necessary to the security of a free State." And then it lays down the law: "the right of the people to keep and bear Arms, shall not be infringed."

The language is perplexing. Does this amendment apply just to people who serve in a state's militia— what we now call the National Guard? Or does it apply to everyone? Arguments about this have raged for many years, but recently the Supreme Court ruled that the Second Amendment applies to everyone. It is an *individual* right, meant for all, not just members of the National Guard.

However, that doesn't mean that the government can't regulate guns. It can and it does. But those regu- lations must meet a strict test. The government must prove that the regulations don't unreasonably restrict an individual's right to own a gun.

The Third and Fourth Amendments assert that your property belongs to you, not the government. The old, much-hated English practice of "quartering" soldiers in private homes—forcing civilians to house and feed soldiers—is unlawful in America during peacetime, and severely restricted in times of war. Your land and possessions cannot be seized, except under extraordinary circumstances. The police or any other law enforcement officials can't search you or take something of yours without a legally sound reason.

Warrants are needed for most searches. These are signed orders from a judge who has seen or heard evidence of criminal activity. With few exceptions, police must have a warrant in hand before they are allowed to search your possessions. They can't go into your house without a warrant. They can't take away your phone without a warrant. They can't listen in on your conversations without a warrant.

If law enforcement officials fail

In Pakistan, anyone who can afford to build a house gives it a six-foot-high wall and a sturdy metal door. When I came to the United States, I was surprised to see that access to entrances is not so guarded. I believe part of the reason is that we Americans know our property and our privacy are protected by laws.

to follow proper search procedures, the search is illegal, and nothing that is found during the search can be used as evidence in a trial. This is called the "exclusionary rule."

The next four amendments are about trials and punishments.

The Fifth Amendment is the longest of these and certainly the best known. Whenever you hear the expression "taking the Fifth," you're hearing a reference to the Fifth Amendment. It means that no one can be forced to testify against himself or herself. You don't have to confess. You don't even have to answer any questions. The Fifth Amendment gives you the right to remain silent.

It also protects you from being unreasonably accused of a major crime. In order to charge you, the federal government must first produce some evidence of wrongdoing to a grand jury. Additionally, the Fifth Amendment protects you from "double jeopardy," or being tried twice for the same crime. It insists that the government can't arrest you, take your life, or seize your property without "due process"—that is, without following clear and well-established legal procedures. If your property is taken for public use, you must be compensated.

The Sixth, Seventh, and Eighth Amendments further describe your legal rights. If you're charged with a crime, or have a property dispute, you have the right to a trial and a jury. In criminal matters, you have the right to a lawyer as well. You have the right to face your accusers, and you have the right to defend yourself. Bail charges, which are court fees that can keep you out of jail while awaiting trial, can't be unreasonably high. If you're found guilty, the punishment for your crime can't be cruel and unusual.

The last two amendments in the Bill of Rights are about the Constitution itself, especially its limits. The Ninth Amendment reminds Americans that our legal rights aren't restricted to what appears in the Constitution. The Tenth Amendment asserts that political power in the United States must be shared among the federal government, the state governments, and the people.

As the world becomes more and more interconnected, I realize that a bill of rights is not just for Americans. All of humanity needs its affirmations of human dignity and its dedication to the rule of law.

MARBURY V. MADISON

DECIDED IN 1803

Who decides if a law is true to the Constitution? What happens when one branch of the federal government disagrees with another branch? Who decides what the Constitution *really* means?

The Supreme Court of the United States has become the final arbiter—the decider—on the constitutionality of laws and government actions. But that wasn't always true. When it was first established, the Supreme Court seemed to have little power. It didn't even have its own courtroom. It met in the Senate clerk's office, and it heard very few cases. The first chief justice of the United States, John Jay, who also contributed to *The Federalist Papers,* thought the position was dull, unworthy of a man of his talents.

But John Marshall, who became chief justice in 1801, thought otherwise. He stayed on the job for thirty-four years, becoming the longest-serving chief justice in the history of the Supreme Court and among the most important people to ever sit on its bench.

One of his most influential decisions came early in his tenure. It started as a minor problem, a bureaucratic slipup that got entangled in politics. James Marbury's complaint against James Madison seemed unlikely to have major constitutional significance. But Marbury decided to make it into a federal case, and John Marshall and his court took up the challenge.

Here was the problem: James Marbury had been promised a job as a justice of the peace in the newly formed District of Columbia. The president of the United States, John Adams, signed all the appropriate papers on his last night in office in 1801. Then he gave them to John Marshall, who at the

John Marshall, chief justice of the United States from 1801 to 1835.

time was serving as secretary of state but had already been confirmed to serve on the Supreme Court.

Marshall, in his capacity as secretary of state, was required to present the papers to James Marbury. Once the papers were in his hands, Marbury would officially become a justice of the peace.

But Marshall ran out of time. He didn't deliver the papers to Marbury. It was an unfortunate error but perhaps an understandable one. The end of a presidential administration is always frenzied, especially when the incoming president is a political enemy of the outgoing president. That was the case in 1801, when Thomas Jefferson took over from John Adams.

The new secretary of state, James Madison, could have delivered the papers to Marbury. But he refused. Madison, an important member of the Jefferson administration, had no interest in giving a plum job to an ally of the Adams administration.

This seemed unfair to Marbury, and also illegal. So he sued Secretary of State Madison.

Marbury took his case straight to the Supreme Court, the highest and most powerful court in the United States. He didn't start first in the lower courts and then petition a higher court to hear his case—he did not, in other words, go through the "appeals process." He started at the top because Congress had passed a law in 1789, the Judiciary Act, that gave the Supreme Court the authority to force public officials to do their job. He believed that Madison was failing to do his job as a public official.

All the Supreme Court had to do was follow the law—that's what Marbury claimed. If the Supreme Court followed the law, then Madison would be compelled to deliver the papers and Marbury would finally get to be a justice of the peace.

Less than two weeks after *Marbury v. Madison* was argued before the justices, the Supreme Court delivered its unanimous opinion. It was written by Chief Justice Marshall, the man who had created the problem in the first place. (Today, a sitting justice would probably recuse himself or herself from the case—voluntarily step aside because of being directly involved. But Marshall didn't have to recuse himself, and he didn't.)

Marshall agreed with Marbury that Secretary of State Madison had been derelict in his duties as a public official. He also agreed that Marbury had been unjustly denied his position because of a trivial timing error.

However, Marshall and the other justices on the court ruled *against* Marbury.

Why?

The problem was the law that Marbury was relying upon, the Judiciary Act. Chief Justice Marshall and his colleagues decided that it was unconstitutional—it gave the Supreme Court powers that the Constitution had denied it.

According to the Constitution, the Supreme Court was mostly an appellate court. That meant that, except in a few very specific situations, a legal complaint couldn't go straight to the Supreme Court. It had to start in lower courts. The decision could be appealed to higher courts from there, all the way to the Supreme Court. But Marbury had *started* his case in the Supreme Court. He had followed the law, but the law was wrong.

The decision was bad news for Marbury: he never did get to be a justice of the peace. But it was very smart politically. Chief Justice Marshall, who had been appointed by the Adams administration, kept the Jefferson administration happy by not forcing it to make an appointment that it didn't want to make. No doubt Madison was also pleased that his innocence was validated by the Constitution he had helped to write.

More important, though, this small and twisty case established what is now known as "judicial review." "It is emphatically the province and duty of the Judicial Department to say what the law is," declared Chief Justice Marshall in his opinion. "If two laws conflict with each other, the Courts must decide on the operation of each."

Who ultimately decides what the Constitution requires in a particular case? Who ultimately decides whether the legislative and executive branches are acting lawfully?

The answer, the Supreme Court asserted in *Marbury v. Madison,* is the Supreme Court, and it's been deciding the constitutionality of our nation's laws ever since.

DRED SCOTT V. SANDFORD

★ ★ ★

DECIDED IN 1857

What happens when the Supreme Court gets it wrong?

Historians generally believe that the Dred Scott decision is one of the worst decisions ever handed down by the Supreme Court—maybe *the* worst. In 1857, Chief Justice Roger Taney, supported by most of the other justices, ruled that enslaved people had no rights anywhere at all in the United States, not even in states where slavery was illegal. The court further ruled that all federal laws limiting slavery in those states and territories that had been settled after the Constitution was ratified were unconstitutional.

This meant that many long-established laws were thrown out the window—notably, the Missouri Compromise of 1820, which had struck an awkward balance between preserving slavery in some parts of the country and abolishing it in others.

Dred Scott, the man at the center of the case, had been born into slavery in Virginia. When he was an adult, he was taken to Illinois, and then into what is now Minnesota. Although slavery was illegal in both those locations, he was kept in bondage. His owner took him back into a slave state, and Scott eventually sued for his freedom, claiming that he had become a free man in those free places.

Scott insisted that he was a citizen of the United States, and that his wife and his children were also citizens of the United States. They had all lived on free soil. They all had the right to their liberty.

No, said the majority of the Supreme Court, none of you are citizens. You are property. Chief Justice Taney wrote that Congress does not have "a greater power over slave property . . . than property of any other description." Moreover, acts of Congress that restricted slavery in the more recently settled western

A portrait of Dred Scott.

lands were unconstitutional. Taney declared that "neither Dred Scott himself, nor any of his family, were made free by being carried into" a place where slavery was unlawfully banned.

The chief justice had hoped that his decision would finally end America's long-running debate over the legality and the morality of slavery.

He was dead wrong.

Although hailed by slave owners as a great victory, the Dred Scott decision horrified millions of other Americans, including Abraham Lincoln. "A house divided against itself cannot stand," he declared in 1858. "I believe this government cannot endure permanently half slave and half free."

Lincoln was elected president in 1860, igniting a civil war between the North and the South. It was the bloodiest conflict ever fought on American soil, and it took almost no one by surprise. Some of the signers of the Constitution, especially those who opposed its pro-slavery provisions in 1787, could see it coming even then.

THE 13TH, 14TH, AND 15TH AMENDMENTS

★ ★ ★

RATIFIED IN 1865, 1868, AND 1870

After the North won the Civil War, it wrote its victory into the Constitution. You can read it in the Thirteenth, Fourteenth, and Fifteenth Amendments.

The Thirteenth Amendment completely abolished slavery. No one could ever again be bought or sold in any state in the United States or in any territory controlled by the United States. It also abolished involuntary servitude—that is, forcing someone to work without pay. Convicted prisoners would be the only exceptions to that rule.

The Fourteenth Amendment expanded liberty to newly freed slaves and to all who lived in America. The first chapter of this book discusses the opening section of the amendment—how it broadened the definition of citizenship and reasserted the rule of law—but the later sections are worth considering, too.

The bitter consequences of losing a war are laid out in the Fourteenth Amendment. *None* of the debts of the Confederate Army would be paid by the United States. That meant that unpaid bills for food, clothing, housing, ammunition—for anything at all that helped the rebels—would be left unpaid. But *all* of the debts of the Union Army had to be paid in full. Anyone who fought for the Confederacy or who supported the rebellion was banned from being elected or appointed to virtually all public offices, including Congress and the presidency. Exceptions were only possible if two-thirds of the House and two-thirds of the Senate agreed to make them.

The Fourteenth Amendment also includes a section about voting rights. It describes the punishments for states that don't extend the vote to all men over the age of twenty-one. (Notice—as many women at the time certainly did—that it was only men. The fight for women's suffrage would take more than fifty years to be resolved.)

The Fifteenth Amendment is simple and strong. A citizen's right to vote can't be denied or limited because of race, skin tone, or history as a slave.

The ugly compromises that the framers had agreed to in Philadelphia were finally rejected in these three amendments. No human being in America would ever again be counted as three-fifths of a person, as slaves were in Article I, Section 2, of the Constitution. No human being would ever be treated as property that must be returned to an owner, as enslaved people were in Article IV, Section 2.

The Constitution had righted the country's greatest wrong.

THE 19TH AND 26TH AMENDMENTS

★ ★ ★

RATIFIED IN 1920 AND 1971

The Civil War enlarged the nation's definition of citizenship in the nineteenth century. In the twentieth century, in part because of two other wars, the privileges of citizenship were extended to every woman in the country and every person aged eighteen and over.

Before the passage of the Nineteenth Amendment, a woman's right to vote depended upon where she lived. In most of the western states, starting with Wyoming in 1869, women could vote in all elections. Montana voters, male and female, sent a woman to Congress in 1916. In Massachusetts, however, women could cast ballots for school committee members, but nothing else. Women in Pennsylvania couldn't do even that much.

By the time America entered World War I in 1917, it was clear that this patchwork arrangement couldn't last. The fight that women's suffrage groups had been waging for decades—with marches, protests, and countless articles and books—was finally winning support in Washington. Four million men were heading off to Europe, leaving many jobs in the hands of strong and capable women. Surely, if America could trust women to run a farm or build weapons in a factory, it could trust them to cast a ballot, too.

A protest in New York City, as part of the movement to get the vote for women. Nearly a century and a half after the Constitution was ratified, women finally had their voices heard and won the right to vote.

President Woodrow Wilson showed little interest in women's suffrage when he took office in 1913, but five years later, during his second term, he was urging

Congress to pass the Nineteenth Amendment. "We have made partners of the women in this war; Shall we admit them only to a partnership of suffering and sacrifice and toil and not to a partnership of privilege and right?"

In 1920, nearly a century and a half after thirty-nine men signed the Constitution, a woman's right to vote was now in it.

Fifty years later, the prolonged and unpopular war in Vietnam was costing tens of thousands of American lives. Millions of men had been drafted into the army, which meant they were required to serve, no matter what they thought about the conflict. As the war (and the draft) raged on, many of its casualties were teenagers, old enough to fight for their country but too young to vote in most states. This seemed wrong to many Americans, those who opposed the war as well as those who supported it. "I strongly favor the eighteen-year-old vote," President Nixon declared in 1970, and he urged the passage of a constitutional amendment that made eighteen the legal voting age in all states.

A year later, after a quick approval by Congress and the states, the Twenty-Sixth Amendment was added to the Constitution.

BROWN V. BOARD OF EDUCATION OF TOPEKA

★ ★ ★

DECIDED IN 1954

"Does segregation of children in public schools solely on the basis of race, even though the physical facilities and other 'tangible' factors may be equal, deprive the children of the minority group of equal educational opportunities?"

This question—read aloud by Chief Justice Earl Warren in the Supreme Court on May 17, 1954—was at the heart of one of the most important legal decisions of the twentieth century. Did the school district of Topeka, Kansas, or any school district, have the right to maintain separate schools for black children and white children?

At the time of the ruling, segregated schools were required in seventeen states, as well as in the District of Columbia. They were allowed in four others, including Kansas.

Should racial segregation be legal in the United States? Can the race of a child determine where and how that child is educated? These questions were sharply debated throughout the country, with public officials in the North and the South largely taking different sides. Within the Supreme Court, there was another sharp debate: Does racial segregation deprive schoolchildren of their constitutional right, guaranteed by the Fourteenth Amendment, to equal treatment under the law?

"We believe that it does," declared Chief Justice Earl Warren, speaking for his colleagues.

After two rounds of oral arguments and months of discussion—and after a Californian, Earl Warren, had become chief justice following the death of a Kentuckian, Fred Vinson—all nine justices came to a unanimous decision.

The Supreme Court signaled a new era in civil rights when it decided *Brown v. Board of Education of Topeka* in 1954. It announced its commitment to protect the rights of all Americans, not just white Americans. But nearly sixty years earlier, the court had sent a very different signal.

In *Plessy v. Ferguson,* decided in 1896, a majority of the justices ruled that racial segregation *was* constitutional. It was perfectly legal for Louisiana to fine

Homer Plessy, a man of mixed racial heritage, for taking a seat in a whites-only train compartment. And it was also legal, the ruling stated, for other public facilities, such as schools, to be segregated by race.

The Fourteenth Amendment, the court decided in 1896, permitted separate facilities for blacks and whites as long as the facilities were of equal quality.

"Separate but equal" became the legal standard after *Plessy v. Ferguson*. A separate train car for blacks was legal as long as it was equal to the car for whites. A separate school was legal as long as it was equal to the school for whites.

But separate *wasn't* equal, and every honest observer of American society knew that was true. With very few exceptions, separate facilities for black Americans were vastly inferior to those for white Americans. Railroad cars for blacks were more cramped than those for whites. Public bathrooms for blacks were shabbier and less sanitary. Schools for black children were held in broken-down buildings with fewer books and teachers.

Justice John Marshall Harlan, who was known for his spirited dissents—written disagreements with colleagues—was the only Supreme Court justice in 1896 to speak out against *Plessy v. Ferguson:* "Our

Constitution is color-blind, and neither knows nor tolerates classes among citizens. In respect of civil rights, all citizens are equal before the law."

Harlan's words fell on deaf ears at the end of the nineteenth century, but they were heard by the court that decided *Brown v. Board of Education of Topeka,* and they continue to be heard today.

OBERGEFELL V. HODGES

★ ★ ★

DECIDED IN 2015

In the summer of 2013, when Jim Obergefell was married in Baltimore, he knew that his spouse was dying. But the couple wanted what little time they had left to be defined by love, not by sickness.

Because same-sex marriage wasn't legal in Ohio, where the couple lived, Obergefell and his partner, John Arthur, went to the considerable trouble of going to Maryland, where it was legal. What Obergefell didn't realize, however, was that his name wouldn't appear as the surviving spouse on his husband's death certificate. In Ohio, his husband would always be a single man.

That was more than Obergefell could bear, so he sued the State of Ohio. In 2015, after it was combined with several other same-sex marriage cases, *Obergefell v. Hodges* went to the Supreme Court.

Thirty-seven states and Washington, D.C., had already recognized some form of same-sex marriage when the case was argued on April 28, 2015; Ohio was among the thirteen that had not.

The court had to decide two issues: Does the Fourteenth Amendment—specifically, its due process and equal protection clauses—require a state to issue marriage licenses to same-sex couples? And does the Fourteenth Amendment, also because of that same pair of clauses, require a state to recognize a same-sex marriage that is performed in another state?

The Supreme Court answered yes to both.

"The right to marry is a fundamental right inherent in the liberty of the person," Justice Anthony Kennedy wrote for the majority opinion. Same-sex couples, he explained, "ask for equal dignity in the eyes of the law. The Constitution grants them that."

LOOKING AHEAD

The Constitution of the United States is now in its third century, and it has aged well. I have no doubt that its future will be just as inspiring as its past. There will be further challenges for our country—there are problems in our democracy that need to be solved right now, and, no doubt, more to come—but I know that we will meet them. Our wise and strong founding documents show us the way.

So far we've looked at my favorite parts of the Constitution, reviewed its history, paraphrased its contents, and discussed important amendments and interpretations. Now it is time for the full text of the Constitution, every word of it. Here, as well, is the magnificent Declaration of Independence.

Afterward, you'll find a few final words from me.

I WANT YOU
TO READ THE
CONSTITUTION

CHAPTER 5

THE DECLARATION OF INDEPENDENCE
and
THE CONSTITUTION OF THE UNITED STATES

THE DECLARATION
OF INDEPENDENCE

IN CONGRESS, JULY 4, 1776.

THE UNANIMOUS DECLARATION OF THE
THIRTEEN UNITED STATES OF AMERICA.

When in the Course of human events, it becomes necessary for one people to dissolve the political bands which have connected them with another, and to assume among the powers of the earth, the separate and equal station to which the Laws of Nature and of Nature's God entitle them, a decent respect to the opinions of mankind requires that they should declare the causes which impel them to the separation.

We hold these truths to be self-evident, that all men are created equal, that they are endowed by their Creator with certain unalienable Rights, that among these are Life, Liberty and the pursuit of Happiness.—That to secure these rights, Governments are instituted among Men, deriving their just powers from the consent of the governed,—That whenever any Form of Government becomes destructive of these ends, it is the Right of the People to alter or to abolish it, and to institute new Government, laying its foundation on such principles and organizing its powers in such form, as to them shall seem most likely to effect their Safety and Happiness. Prudence, indeed, will dictate that Governments long established should not be changed for light and transient causes; and accordingly all experience hath shewn, that mankind are more disposed to suffer, while evils are sufferable, than to right themselves by abolishing the forms to which they are accustomed. But when a long train of abuses and usurpations, pursuing invariably the same Object evinces a design to reduce them under absolute Despotism, it is their right, it is their duty, to throw off such Government, and to provide new Guards for their future security.—Such has been the patient sufferance of these Colonies; and such is now the necessity which constrains them to alter their former Systems of Government. The history of the present King of Great Britain is a history of repeated injuries and usurpations, all having in direct object the establishment of an absolute Tyranny over these States. To prove this, let Facts be submitted to a candid world.

He has refused his Assent to Laws, the most wholesome and necessary for the public good.

He has forbidden his Governors to pass Laws of immediate and pressing importance, unless suspended in their operation till his Assent should be obtained; and when so suspended, he has utterly neglected to attend to them.

He has refused to pass other Laws for the accommodation of large districts of people, unless those people would relinquish the right of Representation in the Legislature, a right inestimable to them and formidable to tyrants only.

He has called together legislative bodies at places unusual, uncomfortable, and distant from the depository of their public Records, for the sole purpose of fatiguing them into compliance with his measures.

He has dissolved Representative Houses repeatedly, for opposing with manly firmness his invasions on the rights of the people.

He has refused for a long time, after such dissolutions, to cause others to be elected; whereby the Legislative powers, incapable of Annihilation, have returned to the People at large for their exercise; the State remaining in the mean time exposed to all the dangers of invasion from without, and convulsions within.

He has endeavoured to prevent the population of these States; for that purpose obstructing the Laws for Naturalization of Foreigners; refusing to pass others to encourage their migrations hither, and raising the conditions of new Appropriations of Lands.

He has obstructed the Administration of Justice, by refusing his Assent to Laws for establishing Judiciary powers.

He has made Judges dependent on his Will alone, for the

tenure of their offices, and the amount and payment of their salaries.

He has erected a multitude of New Offices, and sent hither swarms of Officers to harass our people, and eat out their substance.

He has kept among us, in times of peace, Standing Armies without the Consent of our legislatures.

He has affected to render the Military independent of and superior to the Civil power.

He has combined with others to subject us to a jurisdiction foreign to our constitution, and unacknowledged by our laws; giving his Assent to their Acts of pretended Legislation:

For Quartering large bodies of armed troops among us:

For protecting them, by a mock Trial, from punishment for any Murders which they should commit on the Inhabitants of these States:

For cutting off our Trade with all parts of the world:

For imposing Taxes on us without our Consent:

For depriving us in many cases, of the benefits of Trial by Jury:

For transporting us beyond Seas to be tried for pretended offences

For abolishing the free System of English Laws in a neighbouring Province, establishing therein an Arbitrary government, and enlarging its Boundaries so as to render it at once an example and fit instrument for introducing the same absolute rule into these Colonies:

For taking away our Charters, abolishing our most valuable Laws, and altering fundamentally the Forms of our Governments:

For suspending our own Legislatures, and declaring themselves invested with power to legislate for us in all cases whatsoever.

He has abdicated Government here, by declaring us out of his Protection and waging War against us.

He has plundered our seas, ravaged our Coasts, burnt our towns, and destroyed the lives of our people.

He is at this time transporting large Armies of foreign Mercenaries to compleat the works of death, desolation and tyranny, already begun with circumstances of Cruelty & perfidy scarcely paralleled in the most barbarous ages, and totally unworthy the Head of a civilized nation.

He has constrained our fellow Citizens taken Captive on the high Seas to bear Arms against their Country, to become the executioners of their friends and Brethren, or to fall themselves by their Hands.

He has excited domestic insurrections amongst us, and has endeavored to bring on the inhabitants of our frontiers, the merciless Indian Savages, whose known rule of warfare, is an undistinguished destruction of all ages, sexes and conditions.

In every stage of these Oppressions We have Petitioned for Redress in the most humble terms: Our repeated Petitions have been answered only by repeated injury. A Prince whose character is thus marked by every act which may define a Tyrant, is unfit to be the ruler of a free people.

Nor have We been wanting in attentions to our British

brethren. We have warned them from time to time of attempts by their legislature to extend an unwarrantable jurisdiction over us. We have reminded them of the circumstances of our emigration and settlement here. We have appealed to their native justice and magnanimity, and we have conjured them by the ties of our common kindred to disavow these usurpations, which, would inevitably interrupt our connections and correspondence. They too have been deaf to the voice of justice and of consanguinity. We must, therefore, acquiesce in the necessity, which denounces our Separation, and hold them, as we hold the rest of mankind, Enemies in War, in Peace Friends.

We, therefore, the Representatives of the united States of America, in General Congress, Assembled, appealing to the Supreme Judge of the world for the rectitude of our intentions, do, in the Name, and by Authority of the good People of these Colonies, solemnly publish and declare, That these United Colonies are, and of Right ought to be Free and Independent States; that they are Absolved from all Allegiance to the British Crown, and that all political connection between them and the State of Great Britain, is and ought to be totally dissolved; and that as Free and Independent States, they have full Power to levy War, conclude Peace, contract Alliances, establish Commerce, and to do all other Acts and Things which Independent States may of right do. And for the support of this Declaration, with a firm reliance on the protection of divine Providence, we mutually pledge to each other our Lives, our Fortunes and our sacred Honor.

THE CONSTITUTION OF THE UNITED STATES

We the People of the United States, in Order to form a more perfect Union, establish Justice, insure domestic Tranquility, provide for the common defence, promote the general Welfare, and secure the Blessings of Liberty to ourselves and our Posterity, do ordain and establish this Constitution for the United States of America.

ARTICLE I.

Section 1.

All legislative Powers herein granted shall be vested in a Congress of the United States, which shall consist of a Senate and House of Representatives.

Section 2.

The House of Representatives shall be composed of Members

chosen every second Year by the People of the several States, and the Electors in each State shall have the Qualifications requisite for Electors of the most numerous Branch of the State Legislature.

No Person shall be a Representative who shall not have attained to the Age of twenty five Years, and been seven Years a Citizen of the United States, and who shall not, when elected, be an Inhabitant of that State in which he shall be chosen.

Representatives and direct Taxes shall be apportioned among the several States which may be included within this Union, according to their respective Numbers, which shall be determined by adding to the whole Number of free Persons, including those bound to Service for a Term of Years, and excluding Indians not taxed, three fifths of all other Persons. The actual Enumeration shall be made within three Years after the first Meeting of the Congress of the United States, and within every subsequent Term of ten Years, in such Manner as they shall by Law direct. The Number of Representatives shall not exceed one for every thirty Thousand, but each State shall have at Least one Representative; and until such enumeration shall be made, the State of New Hampshire shall be entitled to chuse three, Massachusetts eight, Rhode-Island and Providence Plantations one, Connecticut five, New-York six, New Jersey four, Pennsylvania eight, Delaware one, Maryland six, Virginia ten, North Carolina five, South Carolina five, and Georgia three.

When vacancies happen in the Representation from any State, the Executive Authority thereof shall issue Writs of Election to fill such Vacancies.

The House of Representatives shall chuse their Speaker and other Officers; and shall have the sole Power of Impeachment.

Section 3.

The Senate of the United States shall be composed of two Senators from each State, chosen by the Legislature thereof, for six Years; and each Senator shall have one Vote.

Immediately after they shall be assembled in Consequence of the first Election, they shall be divided as equally as may be into three Classes. The Seats of the Senators of the first Class shall be vacated at the Expiration of the second Year, of the second Class at the Expiration of the fourth Year, and of the third Class at the Expiration of the sixth Year, so that one third may be chosen every second Year; and if Vacancies happen by Resignation, or otherwise, during the Recess of the Legislature of any State, the Executive thereof may make temporary Appointments until the next Meeting of the Legislature, which shall then fill such Vacancies.

No Person shall be a Senator who shall not have attained to the Age of thirty Years, and been nine Years a Citizen of the United States, and who shall not, when elected, be an Inhabitant of that State for which he shall be chosen.

The Vice President of the United States shall be President

of the Senate, but shall have no Vote, unless they be equally divided.

The Senate shall chuse their other Officers, and also a President pro tempore, in the Absence of the Vice President, or when he shall exercise the Office of President of the United States.

The Senate shall have the sole Power to try all Impeachments. When sitting for that Purpose, they shall be on Oath or Affirmation. When the President of the United States is tried, the Chief Justice shall preside: And no Person shall be convicted without the Concurrence of two thirds of the Members present.

Judgment in Cases of Impeachment shall not extend further than to removal from Office, and disqualification to hold and enjoy any Office of honor, Trust or Profit under the United States: but the Party convicted shall nevertheless be liable and subject to Indictment, Trial, Judgment and Punishment, according to Law.

Section 4.

The Times, Places and Manner of holding Elections for Senators and Representatives, shall be prescribed in each State by the Legislature thereof; but the Congress may at any time by Law make or alter such Regulations, except as to the Places of chusing Senators.

The Congress shall assemble at least once in every Year, and such Meeting shall be on the first Monday in December, unless they shall by Law appoint a different Day.

Section 5.

Each House shall be the Judge of the Elections, Returns and Qualifications of its own Members, and a Majority of each shall constitute a Quorum to do Business; but a smaller Number may adjourn from day to day, and may be authorized to compel the Attendance of absent Members, in such Manner, and under such Penalties as each House may provide.

Each House may determine the Rules of its Proceedings, punish its Members for disorderly Behaviour, and, with the Concurrence of two thirds, expel a Member.

Each House shall keep a Journal of its Proceedings, and from time to time publish the same, excepting such Parts as may in their Judgment require Secrecy; and the Yeas and Nays of the Members of either House on any question shall, at the Desire of one fifth of those Present, be entered on the Journal.

Neither House, during the Session of Congress, shall, without the Consent of the other, adjourn for more than three days, nor to any other Place than that in which the two Houses shall be sitting.

Section 6.

The Senators and Representatives shall receive a Compensation for their Services, to be ascertained by Law, and paid out of the Treasury of the United States. They shall in all Cases, except Treason, Felony and Breach of the Peace, be privileged from Arrest during their Attendance at the Session of their respective Houses, and in going to and returning from the same; and for any Speech or Debate in either House, they shall not be questioned in any other Place.

No Senator or Representative shall, during the Time for which he was elected, be appointed to any civil Office under the Authority of the United States, which shall have been created, or the Emoluments whereof shall have been encreased during such time; and no Person holding any Office under the United States, shall be a Member of either House during his Continuance in Office.

Section 7.

All Bills for raising Revenue shall originate in the House of Representatives; but the Senate may propose or concur with Amendments as on other Bills.

Every Bill which shall have passed the House of Representatives and the Senate, shall, before it become a Law, be presented to the President of the United States; If he approve he shall sign it, but if not he shall return it, with his Objections to that House in which it shall have originated, who shall enter the Objections at large on their Journal, and proceed to reconsider it. If after such Reconsideration two thirds of that House shall agree to pass the Bill, it shall be sent, together with the Objections, to the other House, by which it shall likewise be reconsidered, and if approved by two thirds of that House, it shall become a Law. But in all such Cases the Votes of both Houses shall be determined by yeas and Nays, and the Names of the Persons voting for and against the Bill shall be entered on the Journal of each House respectively. If any Bill shall not be returned by the President within ten Days (Sundays excepted) after it shall have been presented to him, the Same shall be a Law, in like Manner as if he had signed it, unless the Congress by their Adjournment prevent its Return, in which Case it shall not be a Law.

Every Order, Resolution, or Vote to which the Concurrence of the Senate and House of Representatives may be necessary (except on a question of Adjournment) shall be presented to the President of the United States; and before the Same shall take Effect, shall be approved by him, or being disapproved by him, shall be repassed by two thirds of the Senate and House of Representatives, according to the Rules and Limitations prescribed in the Case of a Bill.

Section 8.

The Congress shall have Power To lay and collect Taxes, Duties, Imposts and Excises, to pay the Debts and provide for the common Defence and general Welfare of the United States; but all Duties, Imposts and Excises shall be uniform throughout the United States;

To borrow Money on the credit of the United States;

To regulate Commerce with foreign Nations, and among the several States, and with the Indian Tribes;

To establish an uniform Rule of Naturalization, and uniform Laws on the subject of Bankruptcies throughout the United States;

To coin Money, regulate the Value thereof, and of foreign Coin, and fix the Standard of Weights and Measures;

To provide for the Punishment of counterfeiting the Securities and current Coin of the United States;

To establish Post Offices and post Roads;

To promote the Progress of Science and useful Arts, by securing for limited Times to Authors and Inventors the exclusive Right to their respective Writings and Discoveries;

To constitute Tribunals inferior to the supreme Court;

To define and punish Piracies and Felonies committed on the high Seas, and Offences against the Law of Nations;

To declare War, grant Letters of Marque and Reprisal, and make Rules concerning Captures on Land and Water;

To raise and support Armies, but no Appropriation of Money to that Use shall be for a longer Term than two Years;

To provide and maintain a Navy;

To make Rules for the Government and Regulation of the land and naval Forces;

To provide for calling forth the Militia to execute the Laws of the Union, suppress Insurrections and repel Invasions;

To provide for organizing, arming, and disciplining, the Militia, and for governing such Part of them as may be employed in the Service of the United States, reserving to the States respectively, the Appointment of the Officers, and the Authority of training the Militia according to the discipline prescribed by Congress;

To exercise exclusive Legislation in all Cases whatsoever,

over such District (not exceeding ten Miles square) as may, by Cession of particular States, and the Acceptance of Congress, become the Seat of the Government of the United States, and to exercise like Authority over all Places purchased by the Consent of the Legislature of the State in which the Same shall be, for the Erection of Forts, Magazines, Arsenals, dock-Yards, and other needful Buildings;—And

To make all Laws which shall be necessary and proper for carrying into Execution the foregoing Powers, and all other Powers vested by this Constitution in the Government of the United States, or in any Department or Officer thereof.

Section 9.

The Migration or Importation of such Persons as any of the States now existing shall think proper to admit, shall not be prohibited by the Congress prior to the Year one thousand eight hundred and eight, but a Tax or duty may be imposed on such Importation, not exceeding ten dollars for each Person.

The Privilege of the Writ of Habeas Corpus shall not be suspended, unless when in Cases of Rebellion or Invasion the public Safety may require it.

No Bill of Attainder or ex post facto Law shall be passed.

No Capitation, or other direct, Tax shall be laid, unless in Proportion to the Census or enumeration herein before directed to be taken.

No Tax or Duty shall be laid on Articles exported from any State.

No Preference shall be given by any Regulation of Commerce or Revenue to the Ports of one State over those of another: nor shall Vessels bound to, or from, one State, be obliged to enter, clear, or pay Duties in another.

No Money shall be drawn from the Treasury, but in Consequence of Appropriations made by Law; and a regular Statement and Account of the Receipts and Expenditures of all public Money shall be published from time to time.

No Title of Nobility shall be granted by the United States: And no Person holding any Office of Profit or Trust under them, shall, without the Consent of the Congress, accept of any present, Emolument, Office, or Title, of any kind whatever, from any King, Prince, or foreign State.

Section 10.

No State shall enter into any Treaty, Alliance, or Confederation; grant Letters of Marque and Reprisal; coin Money; emit Bills of Credit; make any Thing but gold and silver Coin a Tender in Payment of Debts; pass any Bill of Attainder, ex post facto Law, or Law impairing the Obligation of Contracts, or grant any Title of Nobility.

No State shall, without the Consent of the Congress, lay any Imposts or Duties on Imports or Exports, except what may be absolutely necessary for executing it's inspection Laws: and the net Produce of all Duties and Imposts, laid by any State on Imports or Exports, shall be for the Use of the Treasury of the United States; and all such Laws shall be subject to the Revision and Controul of the Congress.

No State shall, without the Consent of Congress, lay any Duty of Tonnage, keep Troops, or Ships of War in time of Peace, enter into any Agreement or Compact with another State, or with a foreign Power, or engage in War, unless actually invaded, or in such imminent Danger as will not admit of delay.

ARTICLE II.

Section 1.

The executive Power shall be vested in a President of the United States of America. He shall hold his Office during the Term of four Years, and, together with the Vice President, chosen for the same Term, be elected, as follows

Each State shall appoint, in such Manner as the Legislature thereof may direct, a Number of Electors, equal to the whole Number of Senators and Representatives to which the State may be entitled in the Congress: but no Senator or Representative, or Person holding an Office of Trust or Profit under the United States, shall be appointed an Elector.

The Electors shall meet in their respective States, and vote by Ballot for two Persons, of whom one at least shall not be an Inhabitant of the same State with themselves. And they shall make a List of all the Persons voted for, and of the Number of Votes for each; which List they shall sign and certify, and transmit sealed to the Seat of the Government of the United States, directed to the President of the Senate. The President of the Senate shall, in the Presence of the Senate and House of Representatives, open all the Certificates, and the Votes shall then be counted. The Person having the greatest Number of Votes shall be the President, if such Number be a Majority of the whole Number of Electors appointed; and if there be more than one who have such Majority, and have an equal Number of Votes, then the House of Representatives shall immediately chuse by Ballot one of them for President; and if no Person have a Majority, then from the five highest on the List the said House shall in like Manner chuse the President. But in chusing the President, the Votes shall be taken by States, the Representation from each State having one Vote; A quorum for this Purpose shall consist of a Member or Members from two thirds of the States, and a Majority of all the States shall be necessary to a Choice. In every Case, after the Choice of the President, the Person having the greatest Number of Votes of the Electors shall be the Vice President. But if there should remain two or more who have equal Votes, the Senate shall chuse from them by Ballot the Vice President.

The Congress may determine the Time of chusing the Electors, and the Day on which they shall give their Votes; which Day shall be the same throughout the United States.

No Person except a natural born Citizen, or a Citizen of the United States, at the time of the Adoption of this Constitution, shall be eligible to the Office of President; neither shall any Person be eligible to that Office who shall not have attained to the Age of thirty five Years, and been fourteen Years a Resident within the United States.

In Case of the Removal of the President from Office, or of his Death, Resignation, or Inability to discharge the Powers and Duties of the said Office, the Same shall devolve on the Vice President, and the Congress may by Law provide for the Case of Removal, Death, Resignation or Inability, both of the President and Vice President, declaring what Officer shall then act as President, and such Officer shall act accordingly, until the Disability be removed, or a President shall be elected.

The President shall, at stated Times, receive for his Services, a Compensation, which shall neither be encreased nor diminished during the Period for which he shall have been elected, and he shall not receive within that Period any other Emolument from the United States, or any of them.

Before he enter on the Execution of his Office, he shall take the following Oath or Affirmation:—"I do solemnly swear (or affirm) that I will faithfully execute the Office of President of the United States, and will to the best of my Ability, preserve, protect and defend the Constitution of the United States."

Section 2.

The President shall be Commander in Chief of the Army and Navy of the United States, and of the Militia of the several States, when called into the actual Service of the United States; he may require the Opinion, in writing, of the principal Officer in each of the executive Departments, upon any Subject relating to the Duties of their respective Offices, and he shall have Power to grant Reprieves and Pardons for Offences against the United States, except in Cases of Impeachment.

He shall have Power, by and with the Advice and Consent of the Senate, to make Treaties, provided two thirds of the Senators present concur; and he shall nominate, and by and with the Advice and Consent of the Senate, shall appoint Ambassadors, other public Ministers and Consuls, Judges of the supreme Court, and all other Officers of the United States, whose Appointments are not herein otherwise provided for, and which shall be established by Law: but the Congress may by Law vest the Appointment of such inferior Officers, as they think proper, in the President alone, in the Courts of Law, or in the Heads of Departments.

The President shall have Power to fill up all Vacancies that may happen during the Recess of the Senate, by granting Commissions which shall expire at the End of their next Session.

Section 3.

He shall from time to time give to the Congress Information of the State of the Union, and recommend to their Consideration such Measures as he shall judge necessary and expedient; he may, on extraordinary Occasions, convene both Houses, or either of them, and in Case of Disagreement between them, with Respect to the Time of Adjournment, he may adjourn them to such Time as he shall think proper; he shall receive Ambassadors and other public Ministers;

he shall take Care that the Laws be faithfully executed, and shall Commission all the Officers of the United States.

Section 4.

The President, Vice President and all civil Officers of the United States, shall be removed from Office on Impeachment for, and Conviction of, Treason, Bribery, or other high Crimes and Misdemeanors.

ARTICLE III.

Section 1.

The judicial Power of the United States, shall be vested in one supreme Court, and in such inferior Courts as the Congress may from time to time ordain and establish. The Judges, both of the supreme and inferior Courts, shall hold their Offices during good Behaviour, and shall, at stated Times, receive for their Services, a Compensation, which shall not be diminished during their Continuance in Office.

Section 2.

The judicial Power shall extend to all Cases, in Law and Equity, arising under this Constitution, the Laws of the United States, and Treaties made, or which shall be made, under their Authority;—to all Cases affecting Ambassadors, other public Ministers and Consuls;—to all Cases of admiralty and maritime Jurisdiction;—to Controversies to which the United States shall be a Party;—to Controversies between two or more States;—between a State and Citizens of another State,—between Citizens of different States,—between Citizens of the same State claiming Lands under Grants of different States, and between a State, or the Citizens thereof, and foreign States, Citizens or Subjects.

In all Cases affecting Ambassadors, other public Ministers and Consuls, and those in which a State shall be Party, the supreme Court shall have original Jurisdiction. In all the other Cases before mentioned, the supreme Court shall have appellate Jurisdiction, both as to Law and Fact, with such Exceptions, and under such Regulations as the Congress shall make.

The Trial of all Crimes, except in Cases of Impeachment, shall be by Jury; and such Trial shall be held in the State where the said Crimes shall have been committed; but when not committed within any State, the Trial shall be at such Place or Places as the Congress may by Law have directed.

Section 3.

Treason against the United States, shall consist only in levying War against them, or in adhering to their Enemies, giving them Aid and Comfort. No Person shall be convicted of Treason unless on the Testimony of two Witnesses to the same overt Act, or on Confession in open Court.

The Congress shall have Power to declare the Punishment of Treason, but no Attainder of Treason shall work Corruption of Blood, or Forfeiture except during the Life of the Person attainted.

ARTICLE IV.

Section 1.

Full Faith and Credit shall be given in each State to the public Acts, Records, and judicial Proceedings of every other State. And the Congress may by general Laws prescribe the Manner in which such Acts, Records and Proceedings shall be proved, and the Effect thereof.

Section 2.

The Citizens of each State shall be entitled to all Privileges and Immunities of Citizens in the several States.

A Person charged in any State with Treason, Felony, or other Crime, who shall flee from Justice, and be found in another State, shall on Demand of the executive Authority of the State from which he fled, be delivered up, to be removed to the State having Jurisdiction of the Crime.

No Person held to Service or Labour in one State, under the Laws thereof, escaping into another, shall, in Consequence of any Law or Regulation therein, be discharged from such Service or Labour, but shall be delivered up on Claim of the Party to whom such Service or Labour may be due.

Section 3.

New States may be admitted by the Congress into this Union; but no new State shall be formed or erected within the Jurisdiction of any other State; nor any State be formed by the

Junction of two or more States, or Parts of States, without the Consent of the Legislatures of the States concerned as well as of the Congress.

The Congress shall have Power to dispose of and make all needful Rules and Regulations respecting the Territory or other Property belonging to the United States; and nothing in this Constitution shall be so construed as to Prejudice any Claims of the United States, or of any particular State.

Section 4.

The United States shall guarantee to every State in this Union a Republican Form of Government, and shall protect each of them against Invasion; and on Application of the Legislature, or of the Executive (when the Legislature cannot be convened), against domestic Violence.

ARTICLE V.

The Congress, whenever two thirds of both Houses shall deem it necessary, shall propose Amendments to this Constitution, or, on the Application of the Legislatures of two thirds of the several States, shall call a Convention for proposing Amendments, which, in either Case, shall be valid to all Intents and Purposes, as Part of this Constitution, when ratified by the Legislatures of three fourths of the several States, or by Conventions in three fourths thereof, as the one or the other Mode of Ratification may be proposed by the Congress; Provided that no Amendment which may be made prior to the Year One thousand eight hundred and eight shall in any Manner affect the first and fourth Clauses in the Ninth Section of the first Article; and that no State, without its Consent, shall be deprived of its equal Suffrage in the Senate.

ARTICLE VI.

All Debts contracted and Engagements entered into, before the Adoption of this Constitution, shall be as valid against the United States under this Constitution, as under the Confederation.

This Constitution, and the Laws of the United States which shall be made in Pursuance thereof; and all Treaties made, or which shall be made, under the Authority of the United States, shall be the supreme Law of the Land; and the Judges in every State shall be bound thereby, any Thing in the Constitution or Laws of any State to the Contrary notwithstanding.

The Senators and Representatives before mentioned, and the Members of the several State Legislatures, and all executive and judicial Officers, both of the United States and of the several States, shall be bound by Oath or Affirmation, to support this Constitution; but no religious Test shall ever be required as a Qualification to any Office or public Trust under the United States.

ARTICLE VII.

The Ratification of the Conventions of nine States, shall be sufficient for the Establishment of this Constitution between the States so ratifying the Same.

Done in Convention by the Unanimous Consent of the States present the Seventeenth Day of September in the Year of our Lord one thousand seven hundred and Eighty seven and of the Independance of the United States of America the Twelfth In witness whereof We have hereunto subscribed our Names.

THE AMENDMENTS TO THE CONSTITUTION

The first ten amendments to the Constitution are known as the Bill of Rights. They were ratified on December 15, 1791.

THE PREAMBLE TO THE BILL OF RIGHTS

Congress of the United States

begun and held at the City of New-York, on

Wednesday the fourth of March, one thousand seven hundred and eighty nine.

THE Conventions of a number of the States, having at the time of their adopting the Constitution, expressed a desire, in order to prevent misconstruction or abuse of its powers, that further declaratory and restrictive clauses should be added: And as extending the ground of public confidence in the Government, will best ensure the beneficent ends of its institution.

RESOLVED by the Senate and House of Representatives of the United States of America, in Congress assembled, two thirds of both Houses concurring, that the following Articles be proposed to the Legislatures of the several States, as amendments to the Constitution of the United States, all, or any of which Articles, when ratified by three fourths of the said Legislatures, to be valid to all intents and purposes, as part of the said Constitution; viz.

ARTICLES in addition to, and Amendment of the Constitution of the United States of America, proposed by Congress, and ratified by the Legislatures of the several States, pursuant to the fifth Article of the original Constitution.

AMENDMENT I

Congress shall make no law respecting an establishment of religion, or prohibiting the free exercise thereof; or abridging the freedom of speech, or of the press; or the right of the people peaceably to assemble, and to petition the Government for a redress of grievances.

AMENDMENT II

A well regulated Militia, being necessary to the security of a free State, the right of the people to keep and bear Arms, shall not be infringed.

AMENDMENT III

No Soldier shall, in time of peace be quartered in any house, without the consent of the Owner, nor in time of war, but in a manner to be prescribed by law.

AMENDMENT IV

The right of the people to be secure in their persons, houses, papers, and effects, against unreasonable searches and seizures, shall not be violated, and no Warrants shall issue, but upon probable cause, supported by Oath or affirmation, and particularly describing the place to be searched, and the persons or things to be seized.

AMENDMENT V

No person shall be held to answer for a capital, or otherwise infamous crime, unless on a presentment or indictment of a Grand Jury, except in cases arising in the land or naval forces, or in the Militia, when in actual service in time of War or public danger; nor shall any person be subject for the same offence to be twice put in jeopardy of life or limb; nor shall be compelled in any criminal case to be a witness against himself, nor be deprived of life, liberty, or property, without due process of law; nor shall private property be taken for public use, without just compensation.

AMENDMENT VI

In all criminal prosecutions, the accused shall enjoy the right to a speedy and public trial, by an impartial jury of the State and district wherein the crime shall have been committed, which district shall have been previously ascertained by law, and to be informed of the nature and cause of the accusation; to be confronted with the witnesses against him;

to have compulsory process for obtaining witnesses in his favor, and to have the Assistance of Counsel for his defence.

AMENDMENT VII

In Suits at common law, where the value in controversy shall exceed twenty dollars, the right of trial by jury shall be preserved, and no fact tried by a jury, shall be otherwise re-examined in any Court of the United States, than according to the rules of the common law.

AMENDMENT VIII

Excessive bail shall not be required, nor excessive fines imposed, nor cruel and unusual punishments inflicted.

AMENDMENT IX

The enumeration in the Constitution, of certain rights, shall not be construed to deny or disparage others retained by the people.

AMENDMENT X

The powers not delegated to the United States by the Constitution, nor prohibited by it to the States, are reserved to the States respectively, or to the people.

AMENDMENT XI

Ratified on February 7, 1795
The Judicial power of the United States shall not be construed

to extend to any suit in law or equity, commenced or prosecuted against one of the United States by Citizens of another State, or by Citizens or Subjects of any Foreign State.

AMENDMENT XII

Ratified on June 15, 1804

The Electors shall meet in their respective states and vote by ballot for President and Vice-President, one of whom, at least, shall not be an inhabitant of the same state with themselves; they shall name in their ballots the person voted for as President, and in distinct ballots the person voted for as Vice-President, and they shall make distinct lists of all persons voted for as President, and of all persons voted for as Vice-President, and of the number of votes for each, which lists they shall sign and certify, and transmit sealed to the seat of the government of the United States, directed to the President of the Senate;—the President of the Senate shall, in the presence of the Senate and House of Representatives, open all the certificates and the votes shall then be counted;—The person having the greatest number of votes for President, shall be the President, if such number be a majority of the whole number of Electors appointed; and if no person have such majority, then from the persons having the highest numbers not exceeding three on the list of those voted for as President, the House of Representatives shall choose immediately, by ballot, the President. But in choosing the President, the votes shall be taken by states, the representation from each state having one vote; a quorum for this purpose shall consist of a member or members from two-thirds of the states, and a majority of all the states shall be necessary to a choice. [And if the House of Representatives shall not choose a President whenever the right of choice shall devolve upon them, before the fourth day of March next following, then the Vice-President shall act as President, as in case of the death or other constitutional disability of the President.—] The person having the greatest number of votes as Vice-President, shall be the Vice-President, if such number be a majority of the whole number of Electors appointed, and if no person have a majority, then from the two highest numbers on the list, the Senate shall choose the Vice-President; a quorum for the purpose shall consist of two-thirds of the whole number of Senators, and a majority of the whole number shall be necessary to a choice. But no person constitutionally ineligible to the office of President shall be eligible to that of Vice-President of the United States.

AMENDMENT XIII

Ratified on December 6, 1865

Section 1.

Neither slavery nor involuntary servitude, except as a punishment for crime whereof the party shall have been duly convicted, shall exist within the United States, or any place subject to their jurisdiction.

Section 2.

Congress shall have power to enforce this article by appropriate legislation.

AMENDMENT XIV

Ratified on July 9, 1868

Section 1.

All persons born or naturalized in the United States, and subject to the jurisdiction thereof, are citizens of the United States and of the State wherein they reside. No State shall make or enforce any law which shall abridge the privileges or immunities of citizens of the United States; nor shall any State deprive any person of life, liberty, or property, without due process of law; nor deny to any person within its jurisdiction the equal protection of the laws.

Section 2.

Representatives shall be apportioned among the several States according to their respective numbers, counting the whole number of persons in each State, excluding Indians not taxed. But when the right to vote at any election for the choice of electors for President and Vice-President of the United States, Representatives in Congress, the Executive and Judicial officers of a State, or the members of the Legislature thereof, is denied to any of the male inhabitants of such State, being twenty-one years of age, and citizens of the United States, or in any way abridged, except for participation in rebellion, or other crime, the basis of representation therein shall be reduced in the proportion which the number of such male citizens shall bear to the whole number of male citizens twenty-one years of age in such State.

Section 3.

No person shall be a Senator or Representative in Congress, or elector of President and Vice-President, or hold any office, civil or military, under the United States, or under any State, who, having previously taken an oath, as a member of Congress, or as an officer of the United States, or as a member of any State legislature, or as an executive or judicial officer of any State, to support the Constitution of the United States, shall have engaged in insurrection or rebellion against the same, or given aid or comfort to the enemies thereof. But Congress may by a vote of two-thirds of each House, remove such disability.

Section 4.

The validity of the public debt of the United States, authorized by law, including debts incurred for payment of pensions and bounties for services in suppressing insurrection or rebellion, shall not be questioned. But neither the United States nor any State shall assume or pay any debt or obligation incurred in aid of insurrection or rebellion against the United States, or any claim for the loss or emancipation of any slave; but all such debts, obligations and claims shall be held illegal and void.

Section 5.

The Congress shall have the power to enforce, by appropriate legislation, the provisions of this article.

AMENDMENT XV

Ratified on February 3, 1870

Section 1.

The right of citizens of the United States to vote shall not be denied or abridged by the United States or by any State on account of race, color, or previous condition of servitude—

Section 2.

The Congress shall have the power to enforce this article by appropriate legislation.

AMENDMENT XVI

Ratified on February 3, 1913

The Congress shall have power to lay and collect taxes on incomes, from whatever source derived, without apportionment among the several States, and without regard to any census or enumeration.

AMENDMENT XVII

Ratified on April 8, 1913

The Senate of the United States shall be composed of two Senators from each State, elected by the people thereof, for six years; and each Senator shall have one vote. The electors in each State shall have the qualifications requisite for electors of the most numerous branch of the State legislatures.

When vacancies happen in the representation of any State in the Senate, the executive authority of such State shall issue writs of election to fill such vacancies: Provided, That the legislature of any State may empower the executive thereof to make temporary appointments until the people fill the vacancies by election as the legislature may direct.

This amendment shall not be so construed as to affect the election or term of any Senator chosen before it becomes valid as part of the Constitution.

AMENDMENT XVIII

Ratified on January 16, 1919. Later repealed by Amendment XXI.

Section 1.

After one year from the ratification of this article the manufacture, sale, or transportation of intoxicating liquors within, the importation thereof into, or the exportation thereof from the United States and all territory subject to the jurisdiction thereof for beverage purposes is hereby prohibited.

Section 2.

The Congress and the several States shall have concurrent power to enforce this article by appropriate legislation.

Section 3.

This article shall be inoperative unless it shall have been

ratified as an amendment to the Constitution by the legislatures of the several States, as provided in the Constitution, within seven years from the date of the submission hereof to the States by the Congress.

AMENDMENT XIX

Ratified on August 18, 1920

The right of citizens of the United States to vote shall not be denied or abridged by the United States or by any State on account of sex.

Congress shall have power to enforce this article by appropriate legislation.

AMENDMENT XX

Ratified on January 23, 1933

Section 1.

The terms of the President and the Vice President shall end at noon on the 20th day of January, and the terms of Senators and Representatives at noon on the 3d day of January, of the years in which such terms would have ended if this article had not been ratified; and the terms of their successors shall then begin.

Section 2.

The Congress shall assemble at least once in every year, and such meeting shall begin at noon on the 3d day of January, unless they shall by law appoint a different day.

Section 3.

If, at the time fixed for the beginning of the term of the President, the President elect shall have died, the Vice President elect shall become President. If a President shall not have been chosen before the time fixed for the beginning of his term, or if the President elect shall have failed to qualify, then the Vice President elect shall act as President until a President shall have qualified; and the Congress may by law provide for the case wherein neither a President elect nor a Vice President elect shall have qualified, declaring who shall then act as President, or the manner in which one who is to act shall be selected, and such person shall act accordingly until a President or Vice President shall have qualified.

Section 4.

The Congress may by law provide for the case of the death of any of the persons from whom the House of Representatives may choose a President whenever the right of choice shall have devolved upon them, and for the case of the death of any of the persons from whom the Senate may choose a Vice President whenever the right of choice shall have devolved upon them.

Section 5.

Sections 1 and 2 shall take effect on the 15th day of October following the ratification of this article.

Section 6.

This article shall be inoperative unless it shall have been

ratified as an amendment to the Constitution by the legislatures of three-fourths of the several States within seven years from the date of its submission.

AMENDMENT XXI
Ratified on December 5, 1933

Section 1.
The eighteenth article of amendment to the Constitution of the United States is hereby repealed.

Section 2.
The transportation or importation into any State, Territory, or possession of the United States for delivery or use therein of intoxicating liquors, in violation of the laws thereof, is hereby prohibited.

Section 3.
This article shall be inoperative unless it shall have been ratified as an amendment to the Constitution by conventions in the several States, as provided in the Constitution, within seven years from the date of the submission hereof to the States by the Congress.

AMENDMENT XXII
Ratified on February 27, 1951

Section 1.

No person shall be elected to the office of the President more than twice, and no person who has held the office of President, or acted as President, for more than two years of a term to which some other person was elected President shall be elected to the office of the President more than once. But this Article shall not apply to any person holding the office of President when this Article was proposed by the Congress, and shall not prevent any person who may be holding the office of President, or acting as President, during the term within which this Article becomes operative from holding the office of President or acting as President during the remainder of such term.

Section 2.

This article shall be inoperative unless it shall have been ratified as an amendment to the Constitution by the legislatures of three-fourths of the several States within seven years from the date of its submission to the States by the Congress.

AMENDMENT XXIII

Ratified on March 29, 1961

Section 1.

The District constituting the seat of Government of the United States shall appoint in such manner as the Congress may direct:

A number of electors of President and Vice President equal to the whole number of Senators and Representatives in Congress to which the District would be entitled if it were a State, but in no event more than the least populous State; they shall be in addition to those appointed by the States, but they shall be considered, for the purposes of the election of President and Vice President, to be electors appointed by a State; and they shall meet in the District and perform such duties as provided by the twelfth article of amendment.

Section 2.

The Congress shall have power to enforce this article by appropriate legislation.

AMENDMENT XXIV

Ratified on January 23, 1964

Section 1.

The right of citizens of the United States to vote in any primary or other election for President or Vice President, for electors for President or Vice President, or for Senator or Representative in Congress, shall not be denied or abridged by the United States or any State by reason of failure to pay any poll tax or other tax.

Section 2.

The Congress shall have power to enforce this article by appropriate legislation.

AMENDMENT XXV
Ratified on February 10, 1967

Section 1.

In case of the removal of the President from office or of his death or resignation, the Vice President shall become President.

Section 2.

Whenever there is a vacancy in the office of the Vice President, the President shall nominate a Vice President who shall take office upon confirmation by a majority vote of both Houses of Congress.

Section 3.

Whenever the President transmits to the President pro tempore of the Senate and the Speaker of the House of Representatives his written declaration that he is unable to discharge the powers and duties of his office, and until he transmits to them a written declaration to the contrary, such powers and duties shall be discharged by the Vice President as Acting President.

Section 4.

Whenever the Vice President and a majority of either the principal officers of the executive departments or of such other body as Congress may by law provide, transmit to the President pro tempore of the Senate and the Speaker of the

House of Representatives their written declaration that the President is unable to discharge the powers and duties of his office, the Vice President shall immediately assume the powers and duties of the office as Acting President.

Thereafter, when the President transmits to the President pro tempore of the Senate and the Speaker of the House of Representatives his written declaration that no inability exists, he shall resume the powers and duties of his office unless the Vice President and a majority of either the principal officers of the executive department or of such other body as Congress may by law provide, transmit within four days to the President pro tempore of the Senate and the Speaker of the House of Representatives their written declaration that the President is unable to discharge the powers and duties of his office. Thereupon Congress shall decide the issue, assembling within forty-eight hours for that purpose if not in session. If the Congress, within twenty-one days after receipt of the latter written declaration, or, if Congress is not in session, within twenty-one days after Congress is required to assemble, determines by two-thirds vote of both Houses that the President is unable to discharge the powers and duties of his office, the Vice President shall continue to discharge the same as Acting President; otherwise, the President shall resume the powers and duties of his office.

AMENDMENT XXVI

Ratified on July 1, 1971

Section 1.

The right of citizens of the United States, who are eighteen years of age or older, to vote shall not be denied or abridged by the United States or by any State on account of age.

Section 2.

The Congress shall have power to enforce this article by appropriate legislation.

AMENDMENT XXVII

Originally proposed September 25, 1789. Ratified on May 7, 1992.
No law, varying the compensation for the services of the Senators and Representatives, shall take effect, until an election of Representatives shall have intervened.

STANDING WITH THE CONSTITUTION

Perhaps the best way to close this book is to go back to the opening words of the Constitution: "We the People."

In his famous Gettysburg Address, delivered at the site of a decisive Civil War battle, President Abraham Lincoln reminded his listeners that the American government was "of the people, by the people, for the people." Our Constitution is an agreement *of* the American people that our nation is governed *by* the American people *for* the benefit of the American people. We govern ourselves in this country. We seek the common good.

"We the People" includes you—the young people of America. Your role in honoring the principles of our founding documents may expand over time, but it has already begun. You have an important role to play right now.

Our son Captain Humayun Khan taught his mother and me this lesson many years ago, when he was in the fifth grade. A note came home from his teacher, requesting a conference. *Oh no, what has he done?* we wondered as we headed to the school. We braced ourselves for bad news. Instead, his teacher told us that our son protected the other children from bullies. Whenever a child felt threatened, he or she would turn to Humayun for help. "You should be so proud of him," the teacher said. Humayun was still a child, but he was already fighting back against injustice. He was determined to treat everyone with dignity and respect.

Even as a ten-year-old, he was serving his country.

Our founding documents come to life through our actions. They express our nation's ideals, but we the people need to make them real. When you speak out against religious intolerance, you give voice to First Amendment guarantees of both freedom of speech and freedom of religion. When you vote in your first election, you flex the power of the Twenty-Sixth Amendment.

Here are a few other ways that you can—right now—defend and support the ideals of the United States:

- Read newspapers, watch the news, ask questions. Form opinions about important public policy issues.

- Introduce yourself to newcomers in your school or neighborhood. Let them know they are welcome.

- Speak out when you see injustice. Listen carefully when others speak out.

- Tell someone who is speaking up on behalf of others or whom you see being mistreated that you stand with him or her. Small gestures like this can make a big difference in making someone feel supported. I know they do for me.

- Find common ground between people. I once saw a sign at a Charlottesville high school that its students had petitioned the administration to put up. This sign said something like: HATE HAS NO PLACE IN THIS BUILDING. WE CHERISH THE DIFFERENCES BETWEEN US.

• Research your state's voting laws. Register as soon as you're eligible.

• Talk to military officers, police officers, and other public servants. Explore a career in one of these fields.

• Keep a copy of the Constitution handy (just as I do).

Sometimes, when our nation's principles are threatened, you have to stand up for our democracy. Don't be afraid to be a leader. Be determined. Be peaceful. Never forget your rights or ignore the rights of others. Always respect the rule of law.

America's commitment to justice and dignity is written into the Declaration of Independence and the Constitution, but its most important home is in the hearts of all of us who love this great nation. We may differ sometimes on how to achieve our lofty goals, but all Americans treasure the enduring values of our Founding Fathers.

Every generation has made our country stronger. When I look at your generation—at your kindness, your dedication, your spirit—I see a glorious future for the United States.

I am honored to stand with you.

MORE LANDMARK SUPREME COURT CASES

We've already discussed a number of historic Supreme Court cases—including *Marbury v. Madison, Dred Scott v. Sandford,* and *Brown v. Board of Education of Topeka*—but here are a few more that have been particularly important.

McCULLOCH V. MARYLAND (1819)

Deciding that the State of Maryland had no right to tax the operations of the Second Bank of the United States, a bank created by Congress, the Supreme Court ruled that the federal government has implied powers under the Constitution, including the power to create such a bank—even though that power wasn't explicitly mentioned in the Constitution—and that no state had the right to impede any legitimate exercise of federal authority, in this case through taxation. (Implied powers are those derived under the necessary and proper clause of the Constitution, which permits Congress to make any laws that are "necessary and proper" for the execution of any federal powers set forth in the Constitution.) *Constitutional basis for ruling: Article I, Section 8, Clause 18 (generally known as the necessary and proper clause)*

GIBBONS V. OGDEN (1824)

Ruling that the award of exclusive control over the shipping routes between two states (New York and New Jersey) constituted regulating interstate commerce between two or more states, the Supreme Court held that, under the Constitution, only Congress, and not the states, could regulate such shipping routes. This case, and its reliance on the Constitution's commerce clause, is the basis for bringing much commercial activity conducted between two or more states under federal control. *Constitutional basis for ruling: Article I, Section 8, Clause 3 (generally known as the commerce clause)*

MAPP V. OHIO (1961)

Convicted of violating Ohio's decency laws after explicit materials were found in a police search of her apartment, Dollree Mapp insisted that her conviction should be overturned because the police had neither a lawful search warrant nor probable cause for the search. She argued the search was therefore illegal, a violation of her Fourth Amendment rights. Using the due process clause of the Fourteenth Amendment to apply the protections of the Fourth Amendment when the actions at issue were taken by a state (and not just, as previously, by the federal government), the Supreme Court agreed and ruled that the evidence seized in the search could not be used against Mapp. *Constitutional basis for ruling: Fourth Amendment*

GIDEON V. WAINWRIGHT (1963)

Too poor to pay for a lawyer and told that Florida would not provide one, Clarence Earl Gideon represented himself in a criminal trial and was found guilty. In jail, still acting as his own lawyer, he petitioned the Supreme Court, claiming that Florida had denied him his Sixth Amendment right to counsel. A lawyer was appointed to argue Gideon's case before the Supreme Court, which ruled unanimously in his favor, holding that the states must provide legal counsel for any criminal defendant unable to afford such counsel. This holding re-emphasized that protections under the Bill of Rights covered state as well as federal conduct. When retried in Florida, this time with a lawyer to argue his case, Gideon was acquitted. *Constitutional basis for ruling: Sixth Amendment*

HEART OF ATLANTA MOTEL, INC. V. UNITED STATES (1964)

The owner of a motel in Georgia refused to comply with the Civil Rights Act of 1964, which banned motels and other public establishments from discriminating on the basis of race or other specified categories. He claimed that the law was unconstitutional and that he had the right to rent rooms as he pleased, without government interference. The court unanimously ruled that the Civil Rights Act of 1964 was constitutional, as an action by Congress to regulate interstate commerce under the commerce clause in Article I, and that the owner had no right to flout it. *Constitutional basis for ruling: Article I, Section 8, Clause 3 (generally known as the commerce clause)*

MIRANDA V. ARIZONA (1966)

Arrested and then interrogated for two hours by the police, but never informed of his constitutional rights to remain silent and to have access to legal representation when being questioned by the police, Ernesto Miranda confessed to and was later found guilty of kidnapping and rape. The Supreme Court ruled that Miranda's confession was wrongly obtained because he had been denied those rights and therefore could not be used against him at trial. As a result of this ruling, anyone arrested or charged with a crime is routinely reminded of his or her legal rights under the Constitution, which is popularly known as a "Miranda warning." *Constitutional basis for ruling: Fifth and Sixth Amendments*

TINKER V. DES MOINES (1969)

Suspended from school for wearing black armbands in silent protest against the Vietnam War, five Iowa teenagers asserted that their right to freedom of speech had been violated. The court sided with the young people, famously declaring that students do not "shed their constitutional rights to freedom of speech or expression at the schoolhouse gate." *Constitutional basis for ruling: First Amendment*

ROE V. WADE (1973)

In a case brought on behalf of a Texas woman who was seeking an abortion, the court decided that women had the constitutional right to an abortion, invoking a constitutional right to privacy inherent in the Bill of Rights and the

Fourteenth Amendment. It further ruled that abortions could be performed for any reason during the first trimester (the first three months of pregnancy); that some limitations could be placed on the procedure during the later stages of pregnancy; and that states could ban abortions in the third trimester (the final three months of pregnancy). *Constitutional basis for ruling: Fourteenth Amendment's due process clause*

HAMDI V. RUMSFELD (2004)

Born in Louisiana, raised in Saudi Arabia, and captured by U.S. troops in Afghanistan, Yaser Hamdi was declared an "enemy combatant," and as such, he was held in a series of military prisons, where he was denied due process and access to an attorney. The Supreme Court ruled that Hamdi's U.S. citizenship made it wrongful for the executive branch to have violated his constitutional rights as an American citizen. *Constitutional basis for ruling: Fifth Amendment*

ACKNOWLEDGMENTS

First and foremost, I am grateful to you, reader, for accepting the challenge to be an informed participant in the great American experiment. Our country's future is in your hands. You are the custodians of our magnificent Constitution and Bill of Rights, and the human dignities enshrined in these documents.

I am grateful to Jennifer Joel of ICM for her wise guidance in making this book possible and for her friendship.

I am sincerely thankful to Barbara Marcus and everyone at Random House Children's Books for sharing my quest to bring the story and wisdom of America's extraordinary founding documents to young readers. My gratitude in particular goes to Michelle Frey, my editor, whose conviction and thoughtfulness helped make this book a reality. And to all of my friends at Random House—including Judith Haut, Jennifer Brown, Dominique Cimina, Alison Kolani, Artie Bennett, Stephanie Moss, Maria Middleton, John Adamo, Felicia Frazier, Dawn Ryan, Tracy Heydweiller, and Marisa DiNovis—who have been instrumental in bringing this publication to fruition.

I would also like to especially thank Anne Quirk, who helped me give voice to ideas I feel so passionately.

Thank you, too, to David Webster and Isabel Carey for their legal minds.

I am also grateful to my family for their unconditional love and support and wise counsel. The story of my life would be nowhere without them; they are my light and compass.

—Khizr Khan

My parents were lawyers, people of faith, and fierce believers in human dignity. Working with Khizr Khan has reminded me how much I owe them. It has also reminded me how much I love my husband, my children, and our country. And if all that wasn't enough, Khizr brought the sublime Michelle Frey into my world. This is her book, too.

—Anne Quirk

PICTURE CREDITS AND NOTES

PICTURE CREDITS

Carol M. Highsmith, Library of Congress: 10 (c. 2006),
    90 (c. 2006), 133 (2010)

Gilbert Stuart, Library of Congress: 118 (c. 1800)

Internal Revenue Service: 112 (2016)

Kim Baker, Getty Images: 20 (date unknown)

Library of Congress: 43 (1787)

National Archives Catalog: 56–57 (c. 1787), 127 (1791)

National Park Service: 38 (date unknown)

PD-US: 16 (2016), 77 (2008), 139 (date unknown), 145 (1912),
    154 (2016 and c. 1917)

Warren Leffler, Library of Congress: 28 (1963)

NOTES

CHAPTER 1: WHY WE NEED A CONSTITUTION

21   "No, said the court . . .": *Wallace v. Jaffree,* 1985.

21   "Yes, said the court . . .": *Good News Club v. Milford Central
     School,* 2001.

22   "Maybe, the court ruled . . .": *Zelman v. Simmons-Harris,* 2002.

CHAPTER 2: WRITING THE CONSTITUTION

39   " 'Our affairs,' he noted . . .": Ron Chernow, *Washington: A Life.*
     New York: Penguin, 2010. p. 516.

42   "On May 13, 1787 . . .": Chernow, *Washington.* p. 526.

51   "South Carolina and Georgia . . .": Ron Chernow, *Alexander
     Hamilton.* New York: Penguin, 2004. p. 238.

55   "It was 'little short . . .' ": Chernow, *Washington*. p. 538.

58   " 'I cannot help expressing . . .' ": Benjamin Franklin's final speech to the Constitutional Convention, from the notes of James Madison, 1787. PBS Online.

CHAPTER 4: PERFECTING THE CONSTITUTION

123   "Let us go on . . .": Thomas Jefferson's letter to Wilson C. Nicholas, September 7, 1803. Founders Online, National Archives.

137   "It is emphatically the . . .": *Marbury v. Madison.* Our Documents (ourdocuments.gov).

139   "A greater power over . . .": *Dred Scott v. Sandford.* Our Documents (ourdocuments.gov).

140   "Taney declared that 'neither . . .' ": *Dred Scott v. Sandford.* Our Documents (ourdocuments.gov).

140   "A house divided against . . .": Abraham Lincoln's "A House Divided" speech, June 16, 1858. PBS Online.

146   "We have made partners . . .": Woodrow Wilson's address to the Senate, 1918. History Online.

146   "I strongly favor the . . .": A statement issued by Richard Nixon, 1970. Richard Nixon Foundation (nixonfoundation.org).

147   " 'Does segregation of children . . .' ": *Brown v. Board of Education of Topeka.* Our Documents (ourdocuments.gov).

149   "Our Constitution is color-blind . . .": *Plessy v. Ferguson.* Our Documents (ourdocuments.gov).

152   "The right to marry . . .": *Obergefell v. Hodges.* United States Supreme Court Online.

INDEX

accused, rights of, 103–104, 130, 184, 210

Adams, John, 133

Amendments to Constitution
adding, 15–17, 97–98, 125, 180–181
First, 2, 15–17, 18–29, 129, 183, 194, 209
Fourteenth, 15–17, 30–36, 141–143, 149, 152, 188–190, 210
text of, 182–199
understanding, 101–121, 141–146, 149, 152

Articles of Confederation, 37–45

Articles of Constitution
I, 69–82, 163–173
II, 83–88, 173–177
III, 89–93, 177–178
IV, 94–96, 179–180
V, 15–16, 97–98, 125, 180–181
VI, 99, 181
VII, 100, 181–182

assembly, right of, 26–29

Bill of Rights, 16, 60, 63, 125–131

checks and balances, 45–47

citizens, 31–33, 106, 131, 185, 210

civil rights, 27, 147–150, 208

Fourteenth Amendment on, 15–17, 30–36, 141–143, 149, 152, 188–190, 210

commerce, interstate, 207

Congress (legislative branch), 13, 45–50, 67, 69–82, 113, 163–173, 190–191, 199

Constitutional Convention, 43–58

Continental Congress, 11, 39

courts (judicial branch), 13, 21, 45–47, 89–93, 177–178; *see also* U.S. Supreme Court cases

debts, of government, 99, 181

Declaration of Independence, 9–15, 157–162

elections, 49, 107–109, 113, 118–119, 186–187, 190–191, 195–196

Federalist Papers, The, 61

firearms, right to, 102, 129, 183

Franklin, Benjamin, 48, 52, 55, 58

Hamilton, Alexander, 52, 55, 59–61, 64, 126

Henry, Patrick, 62

individuals' rights, 106, 131, 185

Jay, John, 61, 132
Jefferson, Thomas, 9–15, 19, 60,
    123, 126, 136

Madison, James, 41–44, 46–47, 49,
    51, 59–63, 126, 132–137
Morris, Gouverneur, 55

Paterson, William, 47–48
petition, right to, 26–29
Pinckney, Charles Cotesworth, 51
president (executive branch),
    13, 45–47, 54–55, 83–88,
    115–117, 120–121, 173–177,
    192–198
press, freedom of, 25–26
privacy, 102–103, 129–130, 184,
    209
prohibition of alcohol, 113–114,
    116–117, 191–192, 194
proportional representation,
    47–50

ratification, 58–64, 100, 181–182
religion, freedom of, 19–22

same-sex marriage, 151–152
Sherman, Roger, 48
slavery, 31–32, 50–54, 109–110,
    138–140, 141–143, 187–188
soldiers, housing of, 102, 129–130,
    183
speech, freedom of, 2, 18–29, 129,
    183, 194, 209
states' rights and duties, 94–96,
    106, 131, 179–180, 185, 207

taxes, 111–112, 119, 190, 196
trials, 104, 105, 131, 184–185, 208

U.S. Constitution, 1–7, 65–67; see
    also Amendments; Articles
    Bill of Rights, 16, 60, 63,
        125–131
    Constitutional Convention,
        43–58
    Preamble, 68, 182–183
    ratification of, 58–64, 100,
        181–182
    text of, 163–199
U.S. Supreme Court cases
    Brown v. Board of Education of
        Topeka, 147–150
    Dred Scott v. Sandford, 138–140
    Gibbons v. Ogden, 207
    Gideon v. Wainwright, 208
    Hamdi v. Rumsfeld, 210
    Heart of Atlanta Motel, Inc.
        v. United States, 208
    Mapp v. Ohio, 207
    Marbury v. Madison, 132–137
    McCullough v. Maryland, 206
    Miranda v. Arizona, 209
    Obergefell v. Hodges, 151–152
    Plessy v. Ferguson, 148–150
    Roe v. Wade, 209–210
    Tinker v. Des Moines, 209

voting rights, 111, 114, 121,
    141–146, 190, 192, 198–199

Washington, George, 39–42, 47,
    49, 51, 54–55, 59, 63, 117
women, voting by, 114, 144–146,
    192